THE BALANCE SHEET

88 ESSENTIALS TO UNDERSTAND

FIRST EDITION

Bernard FEVRY
www.mycampusfinance.com

To the reader,

The balance sheet is not only a list of assets and liabilities.
It reveals a lot of financial secrets.
The balance sheet can be transformed into a financial system showing a company's financial position, its financial strengths and weaknesses and even providing a basis for the budget process.

> You are a shareholder and you want to read and understand the balance sheet released by your company.
>
> You are an entrepreneur and you want to read and understand the balance sheet set up by your accountant.
>
> You are a banker and you want to read and understand the balance sheets of your clients.
>
> You are a student in MBA or EMBA program and you would like to review quickly the information released in financial statements.

This book is for you
In few hours, it will help you to assimilate the most important concepts necessary to read and understand a balance sheet.
The book will provide to you case studies to practice and test your new knowledge. It will open to you the access to the fantastic language of accounting and finance.

Bernard FEVRY

You want to go further in accounting and finance?

Many books and online courses are available in these topics

Please have a look at page 112 to discover our proposals and our website: www.mycampusfinance.com

CONTENTS

§ 1 to 7: The 3 dimensions of financial accounting..................................page 5

Why accounting is the language of business?

§ 8 to 17: The origins of the balance sheet...................................page 9

How the concept of balance sheet evolves over the ages?

§ 18 to 25: The balance sheet: visualization...page 17

How a balance sheet looks like?

§ 26 to 37: Accounting principles and process.......................................page 24

What are the main accounting principles governing the balance sheet?
How to build a balance sheet?

§ 38 to 45: Towards corporate finance..page 41

How to transform an accounting vision into a financial vision.
The key role of the working capital requirement.

§ 46 to 53: Building a financial system ……………………………........page 53

What are the 5 key sections of a financial system?

§ 54 to 64: Financial systems' snapshot..page 64

What are the main characteristics of optimal systems, lazy systems and risky systems?

§ 65 to 70: Financial system's evolution over time.........................page 80

How risky situations arise?

§ 71 to 77: Financial systems dynamics..page 87

How to understand the key performance indicators by the dynamics of a financial system.

CONTENTS

§ 78 to 79: Financial subsystems interdependence…………………... page 99

Interconnections and external impacts of threats and risks.

§ 80 to 88: Combinations and consolidated accounting…...................page 102

Theory and practice of consolidated balance sheets

Conclusion..page 112

The 3 dimensions of financial accounting
How the financial information is displayed?

1 What are the main goals of the financial management?

As said Warren Buffett: Financial accounting is the language of business. It is used to show the financial situation of an entity under 3 aspects:

The performance of its activity
The value of the entity
The cash flowing in and out

The company's activity must be efficient meaning that revenues should cover beyond expenses.
The invested capital should be employed rationally in order to increase the company's value.
The inflows and outflows of cash must be controlled to optimize recourse to sources of financing.

So financial accounting provides a clear picture of an organization's financial health and performance, allowing informed decision-making to its investors' satisfaction.

2 How the financial information is disclosed?

The financial information is made public through 3 financial statements:

The balance sheet shows the assets and the debts which allows to get a value of the entity called "Equity"
The profit and loss statement (income statement in US) compares the revenues realized to the costs consumed and computes the income (profit if positive, loss if negative).
The cash flow statement depicts how the cash is generated and used.

The 3 dimensions of financial accounting
How the financial information is displayed?

3 On which period?

The accounting technique uses a period (called accounting period) of 12 months. Usually, the calendar year from January 1st till December 31st is used. But the company could choose a different period of 12 months suiting more its activity.

The profit and loss statement shows the performance and the cash flow statement depicts the inflows and outflows **produced during** the accounting period.

On the other hand, the balance sheet gives a **situation** at the end of the accounting period (called closing date)

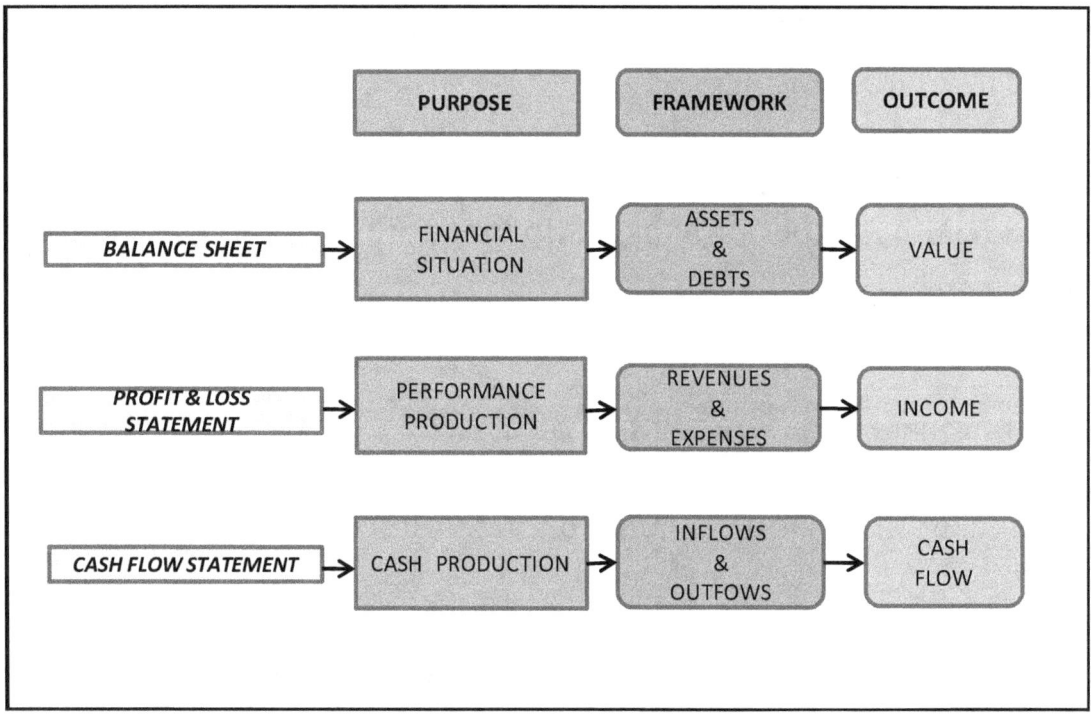

The 3 dimensions of financial accounting
How the financial information is displayed?

4 How the three statements are linked together?

The variation of items of the balance sheet between 2 closing dates is explained by events like the generation of revenues and expenses (showed in the profit and loss statement) and flows of cash (depicted in the cash flow statement).

STATEMENTS' LINK

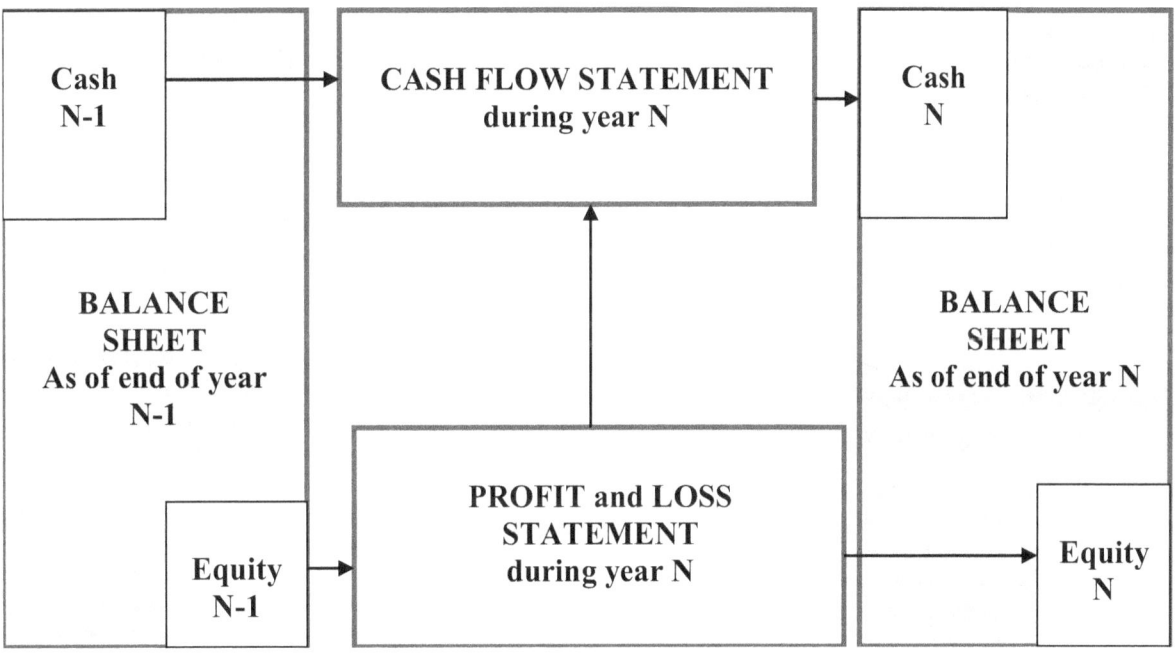

The balance sheet as of end of December year N-1 is also the balance sheet as of beginning of January year N.

The profit and loss statement during year N explains the variance of equity in the balance sheets at the beginning and end of year N.

The cash flow statement during year N explains the variance of the cash position in the balance sheets at the beginning and end of year N.

The 3 dimensions of financial accounting
Towards financial management

5 There are only 3 official statements?

There is a fourth statement: the statement of retained earnings (sometimes called: statement of shareholders' equity). It analyses in details the income allocation decided by the annual shareholders meeting and the exceptional variances of equity like issue of new shares.

6 How profit is allocated?

The net income generated during the accounting period is released to shareholders usually during the 3 months after the closing date.
A shareholders' meeting should be held during the 6 months after the closing date to decide the amount of net income left over for the business (called retained earnings) and consequently the dividends paid to its shareholders

7 Finally what is the link between accounting and finance?

We summarize the link by 3 **R**
The first R is for **R**ecording which is the phase of bookkeeping.
The second R is for **R**eporting the financial statements.
The third R is for **R**eacting after analysis of the financial situation with the help of indicators and metrics.

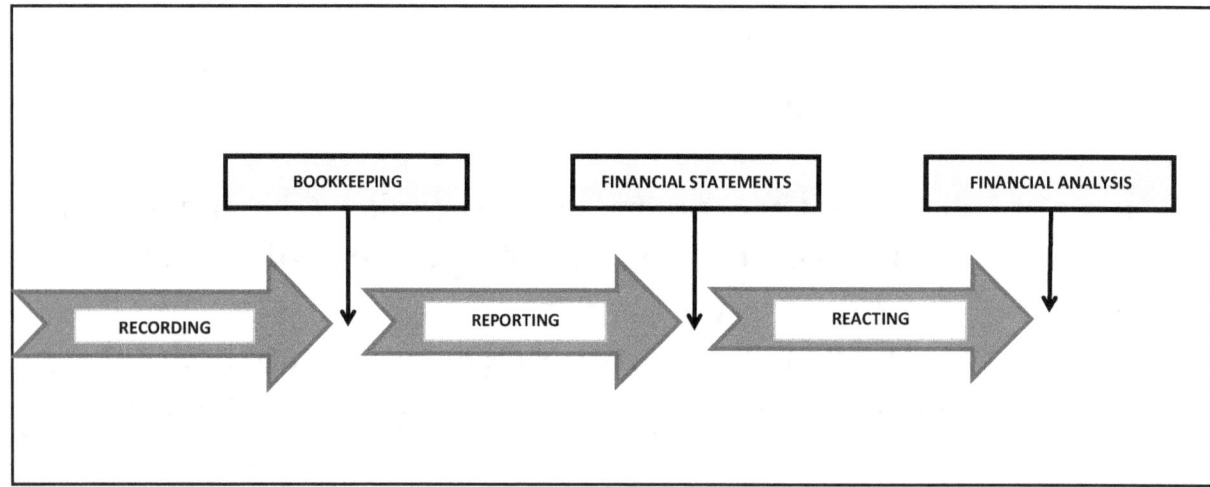

The origins of the balance sheet
Back to the past

8 What is the origin of accounting?

The earliest evidence of accounting comes from Mesopotamian civilization Over 7 000 years ago. Primitive methods were used to record goods purchased and sold.
Later, Egyptians and Babylonians also contributed to early accounting by developing accounting practices and money systems.

9 What about modern accounting later?

In the 15th century Luca Pacioli, a monk living in the republic of Venice, published in 1494 the "Tractatus de computis and scripturis". In which, he proposed a new way to record the business of a merchant: the "T" account.

The origins of the balance sheet
The "T" account

10 The T account: The ancestor of the balance sheet?

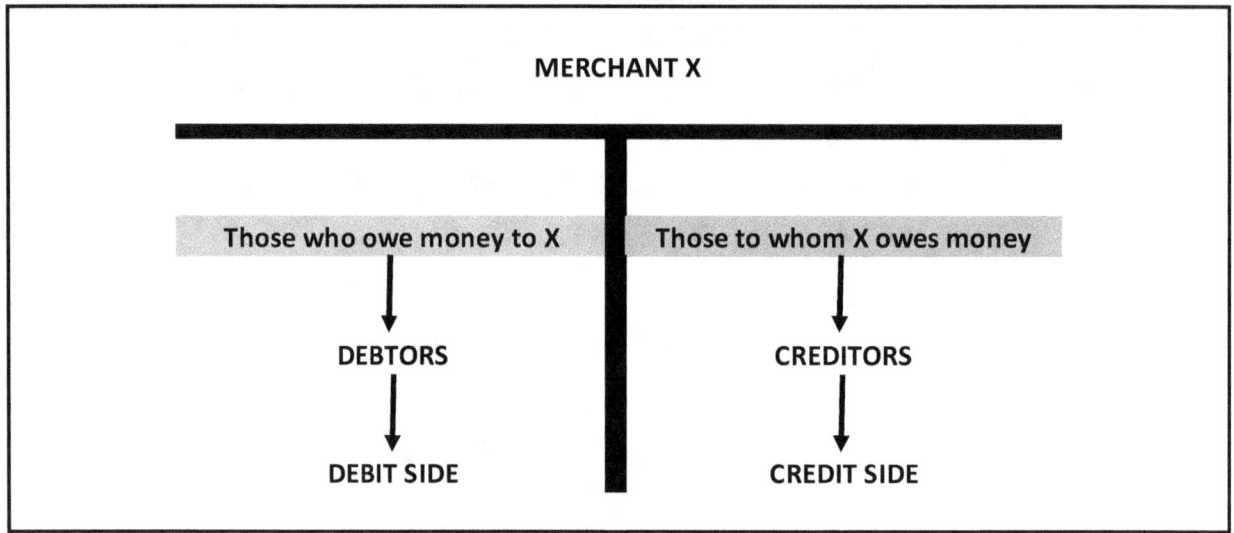

Imagine the large letter T drawn above.

The name of the merchant concerned appears just over the top horizontal line of the T.

The names and amounts of those who owe money to the merchant are listed on the left side. They are called "debtors" from the Latin word "debere" which means "to owe"
This left side is called by analogy the debit side.

The names and amounts of those to whom the merchant owes money are recorded on the right side, separated by the vertical line of the letter T. They are called "creditors" from the Latin word "credere" which means "entrust to loan".
The right side is called by analogy the credit side.

To summarize: the receivables of his customers are on the left side and the debts to his suppliers on the right side.

The origins of the balance sheet
The "T" account

11 How the T account will become a balance sheet?

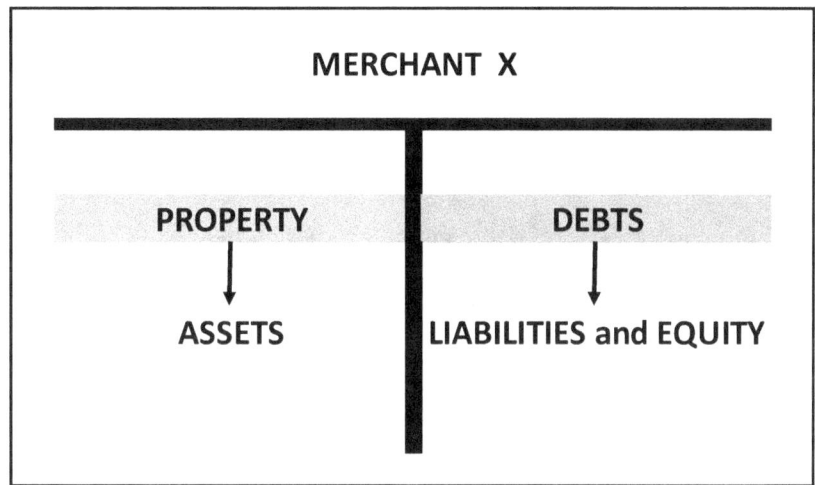

The receivables are the property of the merchant.
But he can also possess other properties like merchandise to be sold, a place to work, machines and some money on its bank account.
The are called "assets"

The same for debts, there are not only those owed to suppliers. There may be bank or tax debts.

Consequently, the balance sheet is an extensive vision of the merchant's business: assets and debts

12 Why are there 2 categories of debts: liabilities and equity?

A liability creates obligations for the borrower:

- ✓ Obligation to repay the amount borrowed
- ✓ Payment of an interest to the loaner
- ✓ Definition of a period of repayment
- ✓ Requirement of periodic repayments
- ✓ Guarantee on the borrower's asset

The origins of the balance sheet
The "equity"

13 So what the "equity" means?

We have to come back to the middle age.

Only one form of company existed: the general partnership. But to participate in it, you have to be merchant.

Then the maritime trade expansion sees the emergence of so-called "sea companies" created for the duration of a voyage to distant islands. They required a lot of money to finance boats and their crews therefore it was necessary to find other investors, rich middle-class persons and nobles who considered trade demeaning. But they could not lend money because at this time the Catholic church prohibited interest-bearing loans.

An illustrious unknown, may be a notary, invented a contract stipulating that rich sponsors (middle-class persons and nobles) entrust their money to general partners (the sea company) in order to go to in distant lands for exotic goods resold in Europe at high prices. This money is a debt but it does not bear interest.

The origins of the balance sheet
The "equity"

On return, the sea company is dissolved and the sponsors get their money back plus the profit made from the resale of the goods and transfer a part of this profit to the general partners in accordance to the contract.

On the other hand, in the event of shipwreck by sea fortune, sponsors and partners lose everything.

14 So what equity means nowadays?

To allow non wealthy people access to investments in sea companies, property titles with low nominal value called "shares" emerged in the 17th century mainly in the Netherland and England.
"Sponsors" became "shareholders" and profits are divided in proportion of the percentage of ownership so the word "dividend". These shares also become more liquid because they can be publicly traded on the Amsterdam Stock Exchange, created in 1602 by the Dutch East India Company.

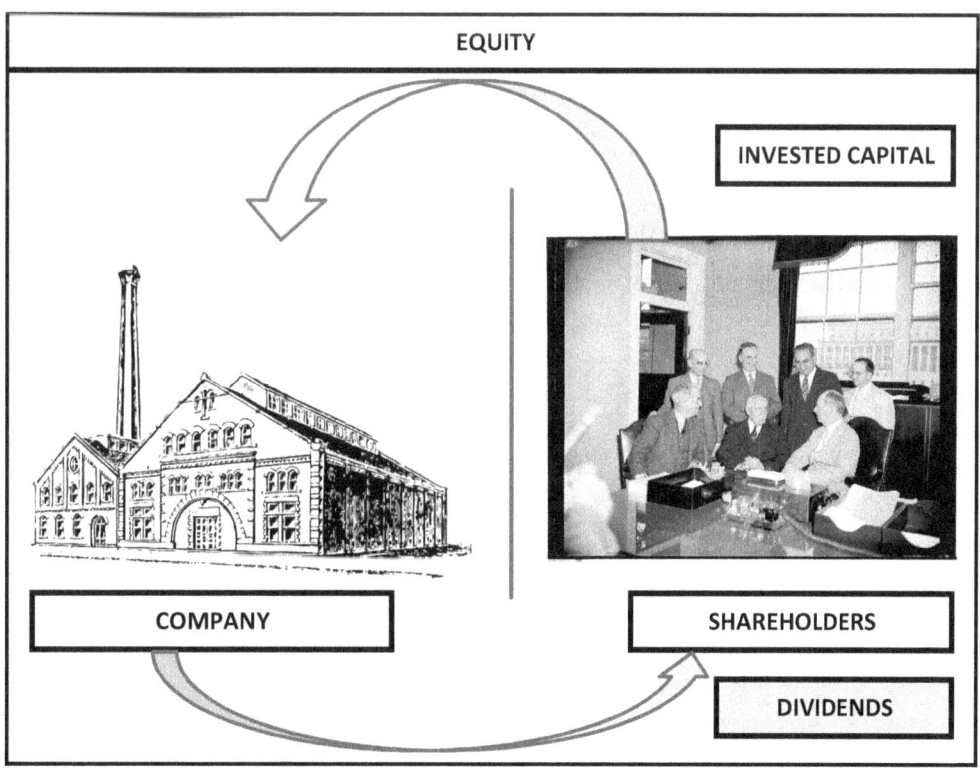

The origins of the balance sheet
The "equity"

15 Why the word "equity" is used for this debt?

Replacing equity in the T account, we have:

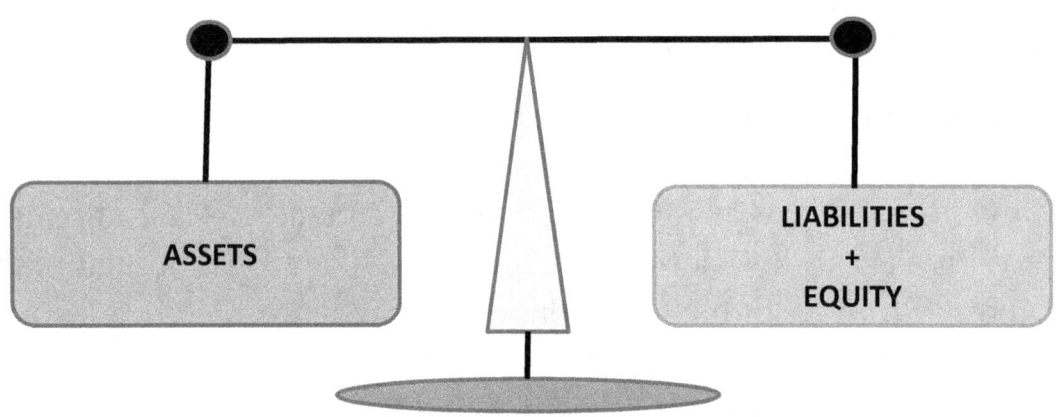

Assets = Liabilities + Equity

That's to say: Equity = Assets - Liabilities

If the company were to be liquidated, equity represents the amount of money returned to shareholders after all assets are sold and liabilities settled. Therefore, equity is also the net worth of a company.

Because equity signifies in a broader sense "fairness and impartiality", we can say that equity, which is the net worth of the company, is consequently the fair value of the ownership interest of shareholders

The origins of the balance sheet
The variation of "equity"

16 How equity varies?

Let's imagine the start of a business.
The owners of a new company invest capital deposited on a bank account open at the name of the company.

At this moment: Value of the company = asset = equity

Value of the company = deposited cash = invested capital

Considering now the situation few months later.
The money deposited the first day is used to invest in new assets (equipment, inventories). More money is borrowed from banks to invest more. Running the business generates receivable not yet collected from customers, liabilities not yet paid to suppliers and cash available.
The present value of the company is computed by difference between the present assets and the present liabilities.

Present value = present assets – present liabilities = present equity

The present equity is different from the invested capital at the creation of the business.

If present equity value is higher than the invested capital:
the company makes a profit

If present equity is lower than the invested capital:
the company makes a loss

Consequently: equity = invested capital +/- profit/loss

The origins of the balance sheet
The variation of "equity"

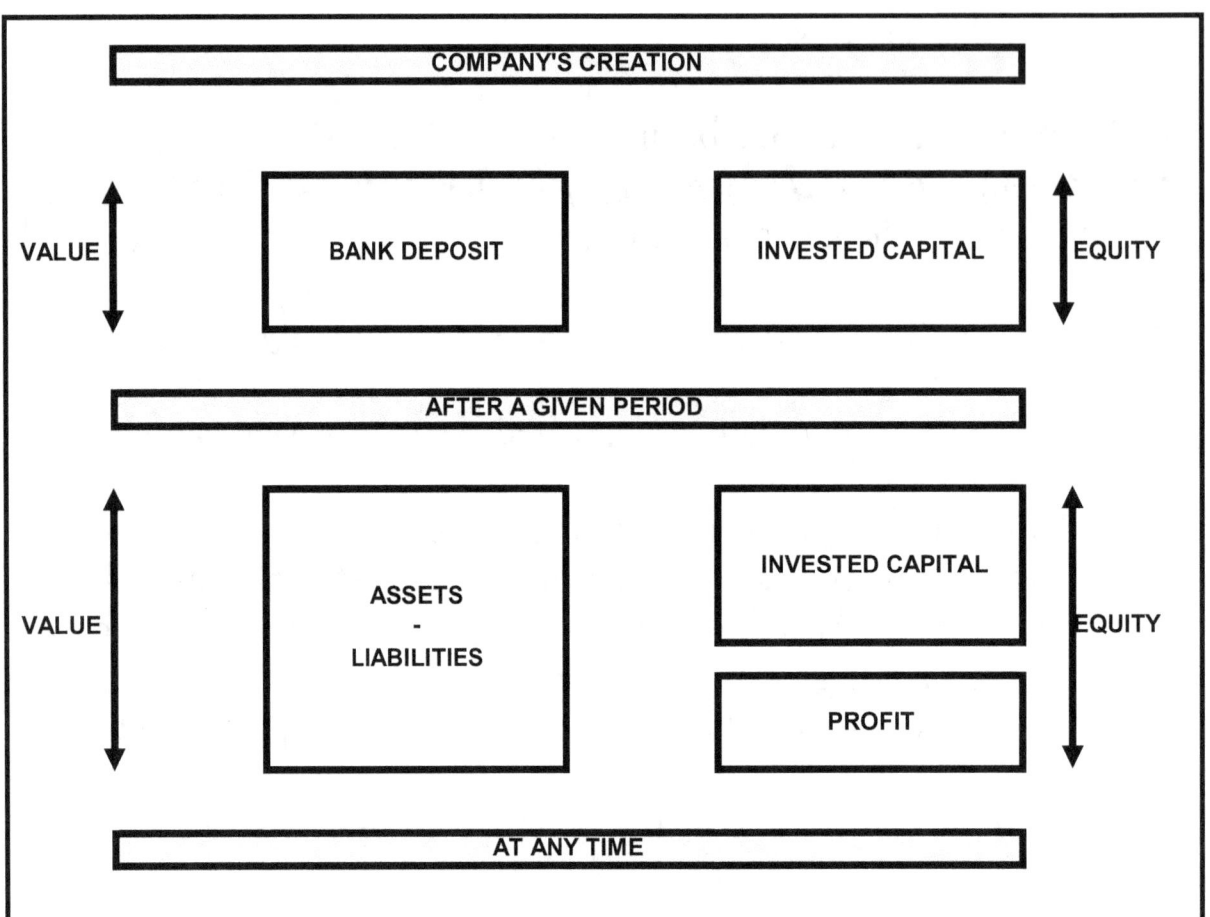

17 Example

The owners deposit USD 10 000 at the creation of the company.

After few months, the situation is:
Present assets = USD 90,200
Present liabilities = USD 70,800
Present value (present equity) = 90,200 – 78,800 = 11,400

Present equity = invested capital +/- profit/loss
11,400 = 10,000 + 1,400
So, the profit = USD 1,400

The balance sheet
Visualization

18 The balance sheet is a table based on the equation:

$$\text{Assets} = \text{Liabilities} + \text{Equity}$$

In continuation with the T account proposed by Luca Pacioli, assets are represented and valued on the left side and debts (liabilities and equity) are valued on the right side.

Sometimes, companies use another format in which the assets section is first shown and the liabilities and equity section is presented under.

19 Here is the balance sheet in the account format according to US-GAAP (**G**enerally **A**ccepted **A**ccounting **P**rinciples in US). The balance sheet is the financial position as of a given date (Called "closing date") which is the last day of the accounting cycle.

BALANCE SHEET as of …/…/…

ASSETS		LIABILITIES AND EQUITY	

CURRENT ASSETS
 Cash and cash equivalents
 Marketable securities
 Accounts receivable less allowance for
     doubtful accounts
 Inventories
 Prepaid expenses
 	
     TOTAL CURRENT ASSETS
 	
 FIXED ASSETS
 Tangible assets less
     less accumulated depreciation
 Intangible assets
 Investments
 	
     TOTAL FIXED ASSETS
 	
     TOTAL ASSETS
		SHORT TERM LIABILITIES
		 Notes payable and bank overdrafts
		 Accounts payable
		 Other payable
		
		     TOTAL SHORT TERM LIABILITIES
		
		 LONG TERM LIABILITIES
		 Bonds
		 Long term bank loans
		
		     TOTAL LONG TERM LIABILITIES
		
		 EQUITY
		 Common stock
		 Retained earnings
		 Profit
		
		     TOTAL EQUITY
		
		     TOTAL LIABILITIES AND EQUITY	

The balance sheet
Visualization

20 What are the current assets?

The current assets are assets expected to be converted into cash within one year. We have 5 categories of current assets shown from the most liquid to the least.

- ✓ Cash and cash equivalent
- ✓ Marketable securities
- ✓ Accounts receivable
- ✓ Inventories
- ✓ Prepaid expenses

Cash is the amount of cash in hand (petty cash) or in bank accounts. Cash equivalent refers to very short-term financial investments (less than 90 days) with a low risk of capital loss.

Marketable securities are financial investments less liquid than cash equivalent since they have longer maturity between 3 and 12 months.

Accounts receivable refers to the bills for sales or services already provided by a company but not yet paid by the customers.
According to the conservatism principle seen further, an estimate should be made during the adjustment process for the amount that is unlikely to be collected. This potential loss is deducted in the balance sheet under the item: "allowance for doubtful accounts".
This allowance is adjusted later at the actual payment.

Inventories lists the cost of merchandise ready for sale in retail companies and the cost of finished goods, raw materials and work in progress not yet converted into finished goods in manufacturing companies.

Prepaid expenses are expenses paid during the present accounting period for an asset or a service consumed during the next one.

The balance sheet
Visualization

21 What are the fixed assets?

Fixed assets are assets used over a period longer than one year by a company in its operations to generate revenue. We have 3 categories of fixed assets.

- ✓ Tangible assets
- ✓ Intangible assets
- ✓ Investments

Tangible assets are physical assets like equipment, machinery, furniture, computers…listed sometimes in an item called: Land and **P**roperty **P**lant and **E**quipment (**PPE**).
They are valued at their purchase cost then adjusted at the end of each accounting cycle according to their use through the process of depreciation.

Intangible assets are non-physical assets like patents, copyrights, trade-marks, licenses, franchises…
They are recorded at their purchase cost. They could be adjusted in case of drop of value through the process of impairment.

Investments are financial securities (shares, bonds) held by the company during more than one year.

Total of current assets and fixed assets appears at the bottom left of the balance sheet.

The balance sheet
Visualization

22 What are the short-term liabilities?

In short-term liabilities, debts incurred by the company, due in less than one year are listed and valued. We have 3 categories of short-term liabilities.

- ✓ Note payable and bank overdraft
- ✓ Accounts payable
- ✓ Other payable

Note payable is a financial debt instrument created by formal legal documents e.g. promissory notes.
Bank overdraft is a credit granted by a bank during a short period of time and up to a maximum of amount.

Accounts payable represent the total of invoices from the suppliers for the purchase of goods and services already received and not yet paid. It is a form of credit allowed by suppliers.

Other payable refers to payable due to other creditors than suppliers like employees (salaries), government (taxes), shareholders (dividends)...

The balance sheet
Visualization

23 What are the long-term liabilities?

Long-term liabilities are mainly financial debt due in more than one year. We have 2 categories of long-term liabilities

- ✓ Bonds
- ✓ Long-term bank loans

Bonds are financial instrument issued by a company in order to raise money from public for a set period of time. In return, the company pays interest (called coupon) at regular intervals and repays the nominal value of the bond when it matures.

Long-term bank loans issued by banks. The portion of long-term liabilities (called current portion) to be repaid in less than one year is categorized as a short-term liability.
The list includes also long-term leases that have been capitalized.

24 At last we have Equity

The owner's equity (single ownership company) or shareholders' equity is the net worth of the company given by difference between assets and liabilities and is also the sum of invested capital.
We have 3 categories.

- ✓ Shareholders' equity
- ✓ Retained earnings
- ✓ Profit or loss

Shareholders' equity is called Common stock (US) or Capital (GB). Equity capital comes in the form of cash in exchange for company ownership, usually through shares (stocks in US).
Owning shares gives the right to part of annual profit called dividends.

The balance sheet
Visualization

Retained earnings (US) or Reserve (GB) is the portion of the profit from the former years, not paid as dividends so kept in the company (like a reinvestment) by decision of shareholders.

Profit or loss refers to the financial outcome of a business's operations over the last period of 12 months (accounting cycle). It summarizes the financial performance of the company by difference between its revenues and its expenses.
Details are gathered in another statement called "Profit and loss statement" or "Income statement" in US.

After shareholders annual meeting (held a maximum of 6 months after the closing date), the income is allocated to certain balance sheet items.

Profit is shared between retained earnings and dividends payable according to the distribution of profit decided by the shareholders. Loss is deducted from the existing retained earnings or from the common stock.

Total of short-term liabilities, long-term liabilities and equity appears at the bottom right of the balance sheet.
By definition, the balance sheet is balanced.

More information? Please refer to our book:
"The profit and loss statement: 88 essentials to understand" available at AMAZON

The balance sheet
Visualization

25 What the IFRS format?

According to IFRS (**I**nternational **F**inancial **R**eporting **S**tandards), the assets are shown from the least liquid at the top (non-current assets like tangible assets) to the most liquid i.e. cash (in current assets). On the right-hand side, equity is listed before the long-term liabilities (called non-current liabilities) and the short-term liabilities (called current liabilities)

BALANCE SHEET as of …/…/…

ASSETS		EQUITY and LIABILITIES	
NON CURRENT ASSETS Tangible assets less accumulated depreciation Intangible assets Investments **TOTAL NON CURRENT ASSETS** **CURRENT ASSETS** Inventories Trade receivable Marketable securities Cash and cash equivalent **TOTAL CURRENT ASSETS** **TOTAL ASSETS**		**EQUITY** Share capital Reserve Non-distributable reserve **TOTAL EQUITY** **NON-CURRENT LIABILITIES** Emprunts Provisions **TOTAL NON-CURRENT LIABILITIES** **CURRENT LIABILITIES** Trade creditors Other creditors Short-term loans **TOTAL CURRENT LIABILITIES** **TOTAL EQUITY AND LIABILITIES**	

Accounting principles and process
History of accounting principles

26 why we have accounting principles?

If we consider that accounting looks like a language useful to depict the financial situation of a company, the accounting principles can be assimilated to the grammar rules necessary to speak a correct language.

27 History of the accounting principles

During the 18th and 19th centuries, the industrial revolution, particularly in the USA, saw the appearance of numerous companies seeking investors.
These wanted reliable and comparable financial statements in order to choose the safest or most profitable investments.
All of this leaded to the need for standardized accounting practices, a formal accounting education and professional bodies
This is why it was decided to organize the profession of accountant and to create in 1896 the diploma of "Certified Public Accountant" i.e. people independent of a company and responsible of reviewing its accounts

Accounting principles and process
The balance sheet's basic accounting principles

28 What are the 2 main accounting principles?

The balance sheet is governed by two main accounting principles:

- ✓ Historical cost principle
- ✓ Conservatism principle

According to the historical cost principle, assets and liabilities are recorded at their value when first acquired.
The relevance of this principle is driven by the necessity to provide consistent and comparable financial reports over the years. Consequently, the values of assets often differ from their current market value. That's why equity, the value of the company, cannot described as market value but "book value" of the company.
"book" meaning "given by accounting books"

Through the conservatism principle, the accountant must recognize a loss on an asset or a debt even if there is an uncertainty about the outcome whereas profit is only recognized when it is assured of being received.
Different types of assets are especially concerned: tangible and intangible fixed assets, inventories and accounts receivable.

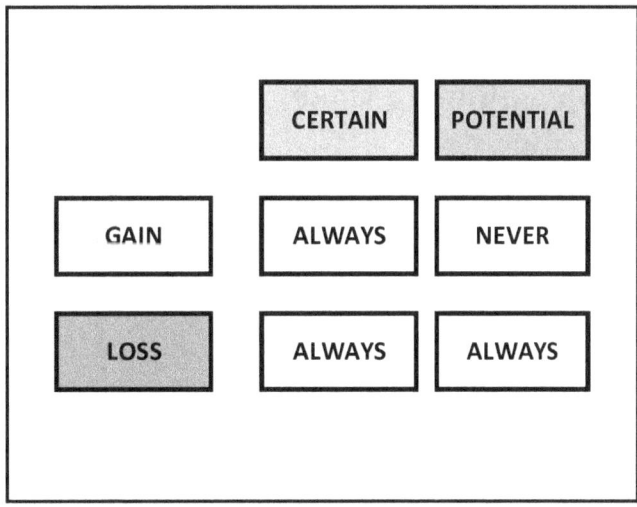

Accounting principles and process
The balance sheet's other accounting principles

29 What about other principles?

The full disclosure principle ensures that all relevant information impacting financial results or financial position is disclosed in notes to financial statements (like changes in accounting policies, reason for impairment, existing litigation…)

The monetary unit principle states that business transactions should only be expressed in only one currency which leads to foreign exchange costs and revenues for international companies.

The consistency principle ensures that financial statements remain comparable over time, allowing stakeholders to identify trends and make informed decisions.
If a change in accounting principle or method is necessary, the notes to financial statements should inform the cause and the consequence of the change and especially the impact on the profit of the company.

Accounting principles and process
The accounting process

30 How the accountant builds a balance sheet?

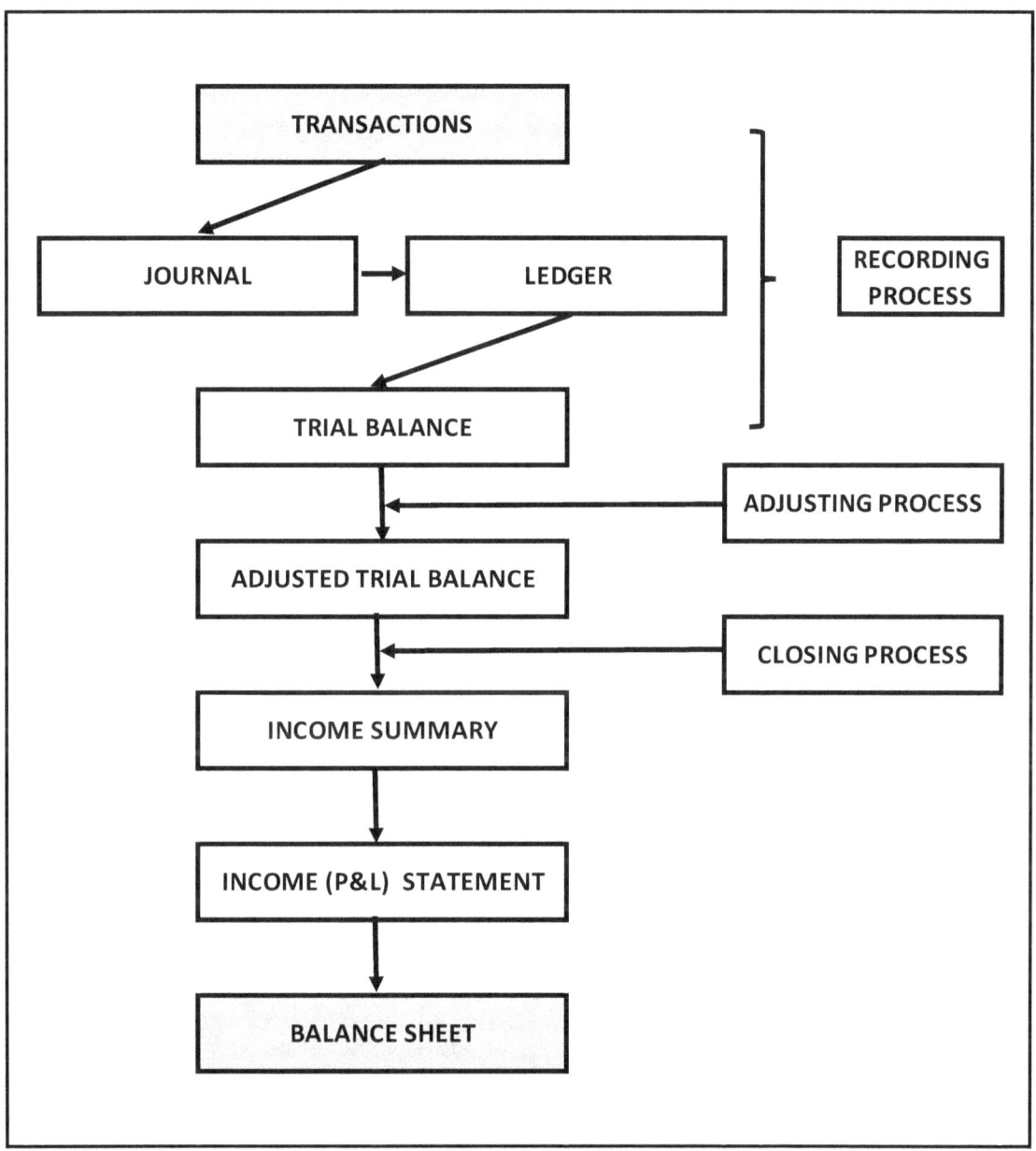

The full process is divided into 3 phases.

- ✓ The recording process
- ✓ The adjusting process
- ✓ The closing process

Accounting principles and process
The accounting process

31 The recording process:

The accountant does not make a balance sheet after each transaction. Every item of the balance sheet is represented by a simple account called T account having also a two-sides structure but at another scale.

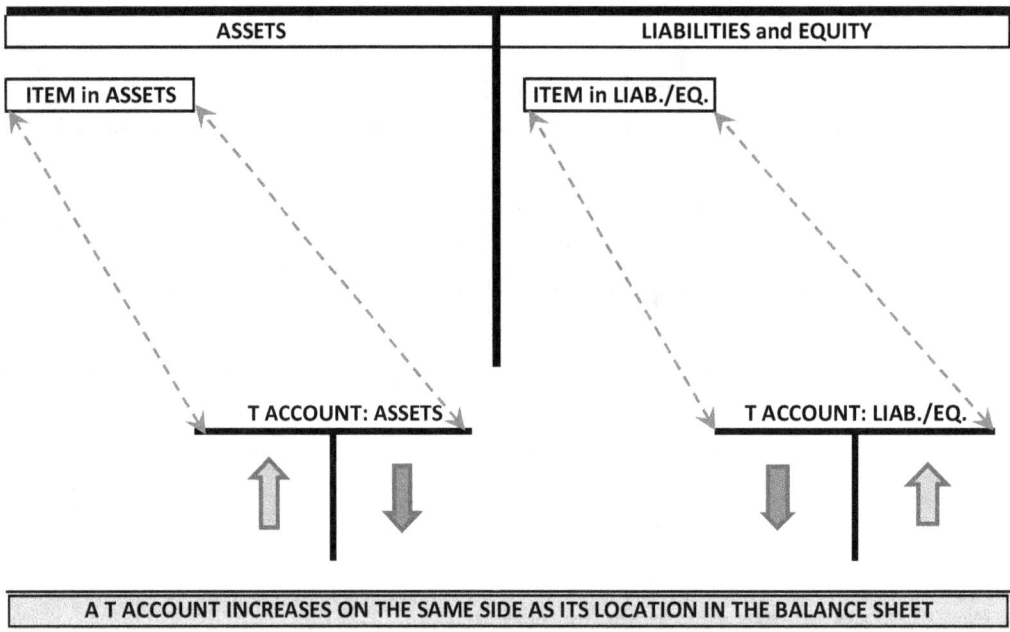

The two-sides structure of a T account has been seen in § 10 page 10.

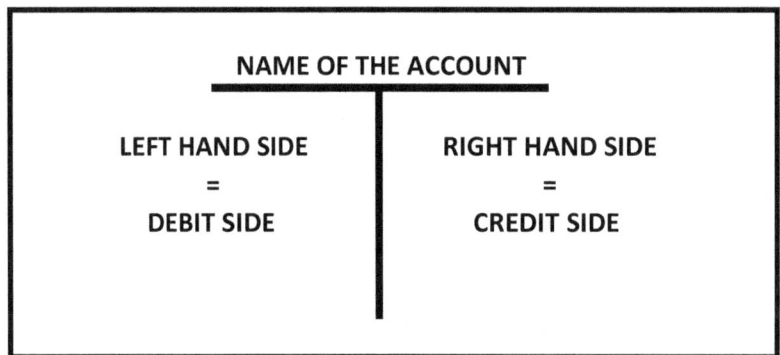

So, the T account rule is: An account belonging to assets is debited (left hand side) when it increases and credited (right hand side) when it decreases.

Accounting principles and process
The accounting process

An account belonging to liabilities or equity is credited (right hand side) when it increases and debited (left hand side) when it decreases. Don't think about your bank statement for which the debit is bad news and credit is good news!!!

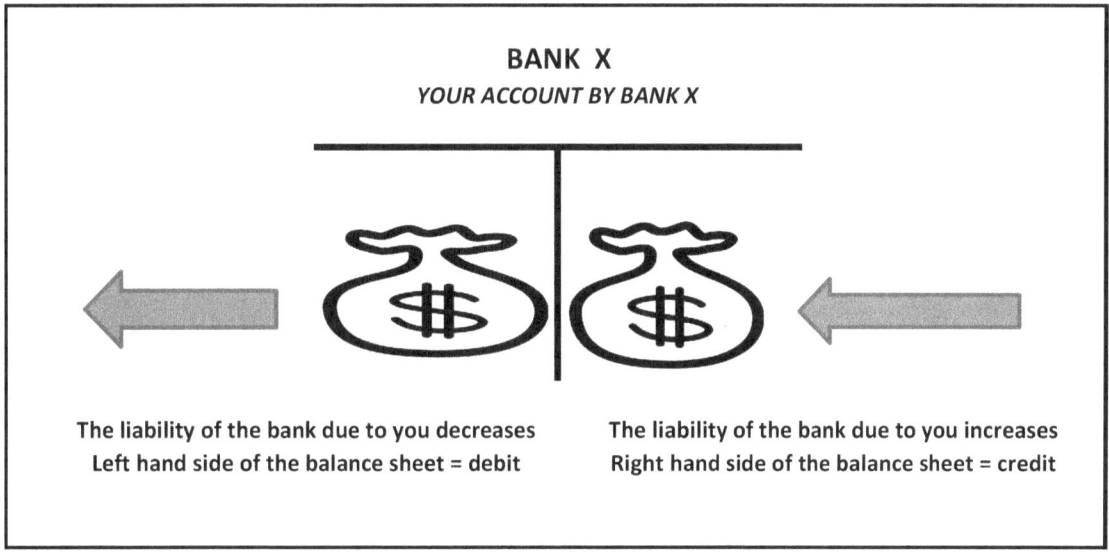

The statement received from the bank comes from its accounting in which your money is a liability due to you.

Now, let's move on to the transaction recording process.

Initially, all financial transactions are recorded in chronological order in a book called the journal.
Since Luca Pacioli (Refer to § 9 page 9), a double-entry bookkeeping system is applied in which each transaction affects at least two accounts to keep the accounting equation: Assets = liabilities + equity.

The total debits should always equal the total credits.

To comply with reporting standards, each account is assigned to an identification number in a chart of accounts listed by categories (current assets, fixed assets, short-term liabilities, long-term liabilities, equity) defined at the national or international level.

Accounting principles and process
The accounting process

		GENERAL JOURNAL		
		Period: from July 1st till July 31st		
Date	Posting	ACCOUNTS TITLES AND EXPLANATION	DEBIT	CREDIT
JUL 1st	100	CASH AT BANK	10 000	
	310	COMMON STOCK		10 000
		To record initial investment of Mr X Shareholder		
JUL 15th	105	MERCHANDISE INVENTORY	4 500	
	201001	ACCOUNT PAYABLE YCM COMPANY		4 500
		To record purchase of inventory invoice 13/124		
JUL 31st	202001	ACCOUNT PAYABLE YCM COMPANY	2 500	
	100	CASH AT BANK		2 500
		To record a partial payment of inventory invoice 13/124		
		TOTAL	17 000	17 000

These journal entries are then posted to the ledger, which is a book collecting the accounts. It shows the changes made to each account as a result of the transactions.

The account in the ledger is an extension of the T account

	LEDGER OF CASH AT BANK ACCOUNT N° 100				
	Period from July 1st till July 31st				
		SUMS		BALANCE	
Date	EXPLANATION	DEBIT	CREDIT	DEBIT	CREDIT
JUL 1st	*Initial investment of Mr X Shareholder*	10 000		10 000	
JUL 31st	*Partial payment of inventory invoice YCM 13/124*		2 500	7 500	
	TOTAL	10 000	2 500	7 500	

Accounting principles and process
The accounting process

The trial balance is a bookkeeping worksheet that lists the sums and the balances of all ledger accounts in two columns: one for debits and one for credits.

ACC N°	ACCOUNT TITLE	SUMS DEBIT	SUMS CREDIT	BALANCE DEBIT	BALANCE CREDIT
	TRIAL BALANCE as of JULY 31st				
100	CASH	10 000	2 500	7 500	
105	MERCHANDISE INVENTORY	4 500		4 500	
201	ACCOUNT PAYABLE	2 500	4 500		2 000
310	COMMON STOCK		10 000		10 000
	TOTAL	17 000	17 000	12 000	12 000

A trial balance is prepared periodically, usually at the end of every reporting period.

A trial balance is used to detect some accounting errors and is the first step in an audit procedure before moving on to more complex and detailed analyses.

More information? Please refer to our book "The 88 essentials an MBA student must know in financial accounting" available i AMAZON.

Accounting principles and process
The accounting process

32 The adjusting process:

The accounts should reflect a fair and true view of the financial situation of a company. An adjustment process is needed at the end of each accounting period to check the respect of accounting principles in order to prepare consistent statements.

- ✓ Matching principle
- ✓ Conservatism principle

These principles are also governing the profit and loss statement. So, to get a full information, please refer to our book: "The profit and loss statement: 88 essentials to understand" available at AMAZON

To illustrate the consequences on the balance sheet, four categories of adjustments are developed below.

- ✓ Inventory physical counting
- ✓ Depreciation calculation
- ✓ Assets and liabilities revaluation
- ✓ Adjustment of revenues and expenses

Accounting principles and process
The accounting process

33 Inventory physical counting

According to the matching principle, the direct cost of goods proposed by a company are recorded in inventories when they are purchased or produced without any consequence on the profit or loss.

When the goods are sold, their cost is recorded according to the equation:

$$\text{Cost of goods sold} = \text{beginning period inventory} + \text{purchase} - \text{ending period inventory}$$

Consequently, a physical count of the quantities and values of inventories is performed in order to calculate the gross margin by difference between sales and cost of goods during a period.

Even if a perpetual inventory tracking system calculates after each sale the quantity and the cost of goods on hand, errors and theft could happen. Also, recourse to a random physical count must be carried out from time to time.

Accounting principles and process
The accounting process

34 Depreciation calculation

The matching principle defines that profit or loss of a company during a period is calculated as the balance between the revenues realized during the period and the expenses occurred during the same period.

For capital expenses (e.g. fixed tangible assets) likely generating revenues over multiple periods, the expense is allocated by period according to its use. This cost is called the depreciation expense for the period.

The value of the fixed tangible asset is reduced accordingly.

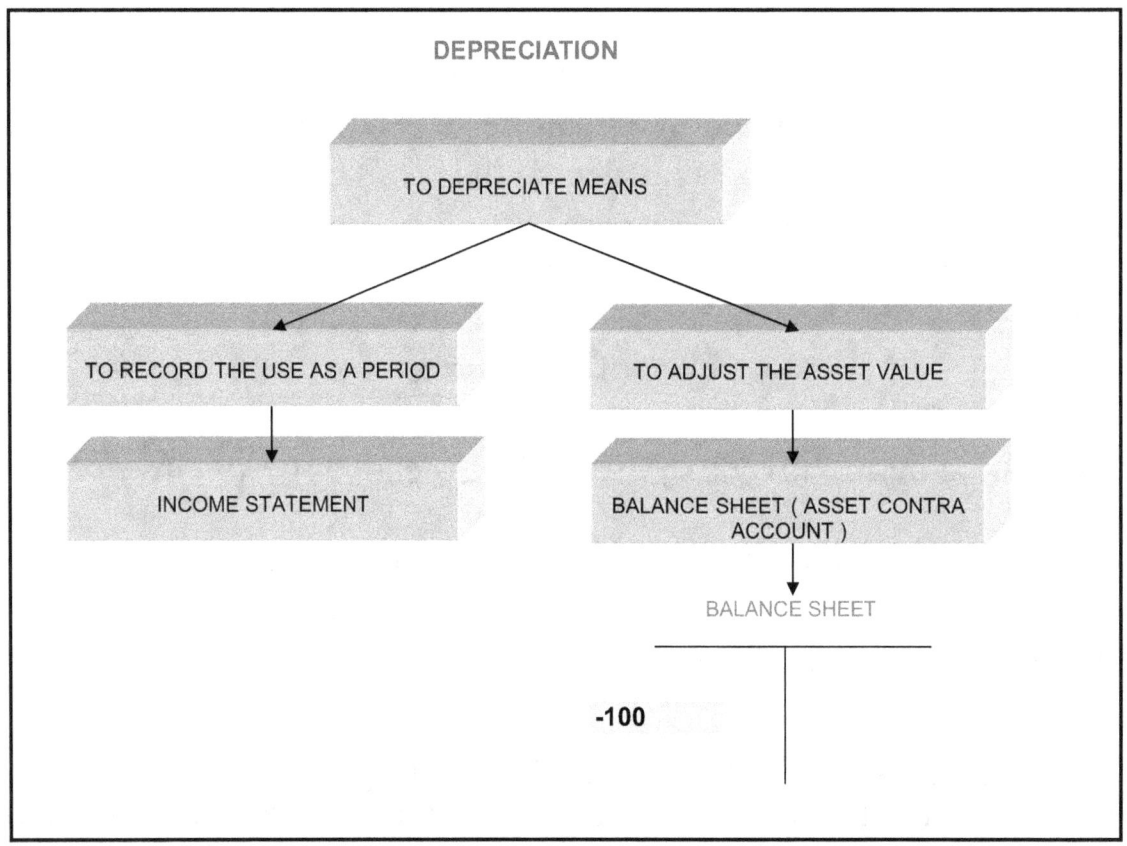

The yearly depreciation decreases the asset value. It is deducted from the gross value (historical cost) of the asset on the left-hand side of the balance sheet and calculated according to different methods.

Accounting principles and process
The accounting process

The most common are:

- ✓ The straight-line method which spreads the cost of the asset over its useful life.
- ✓ The double declining method is an accelerated depreciation way leading to a higher depreciation expense in the earlier years of the asset's life.

The land is never depreciated because it is considered to have an indefinite useful life. But, In US accounting, when a land is operated for mineral extraction, its decrease of value is recorded by the way of "Depletion"

Some intangible assets such as patents, copyrights, trademarks and goodwill, are amortized rather than depreciated. The most common method is the straight-line method. The useful life is often determined by legal or contractual terms. (e.g. 20 years for a patent)

To get a full information about depreciation calculations, please refer to our book: "The profit and loss statement: 88 essentials to understand" available at AMAZON

Accounting principles and process
The accounting process

35 Assets and liabilities revaluations

Assets must be reevaluated to their fair value in the accounting books. But the conservatism principle (refer to § 28 page 25) enforces some limits:

- ✓ Upward potential revaluation is not permitted, (except in case of hyperinflation by balancing the revaluation with a special reserve non-distributable to shareholders).
- ✓ Downward revaluation (called impairment) is mandatory if the book value of an asset is carrying an amount higher than its recoverable value.

The impairment is called "allowance" (e.g. allowance for doubtful accounts) and recorded by a negative item (contra account) in assets on the left-hand side.
Liabilities are also concerned in case of a possible higher repayment in the future (e.g. in case of the variance of the exchange rate of a debt negotiated in foreign currency).
An adjustment of the liability is necessary on the right-hand side.

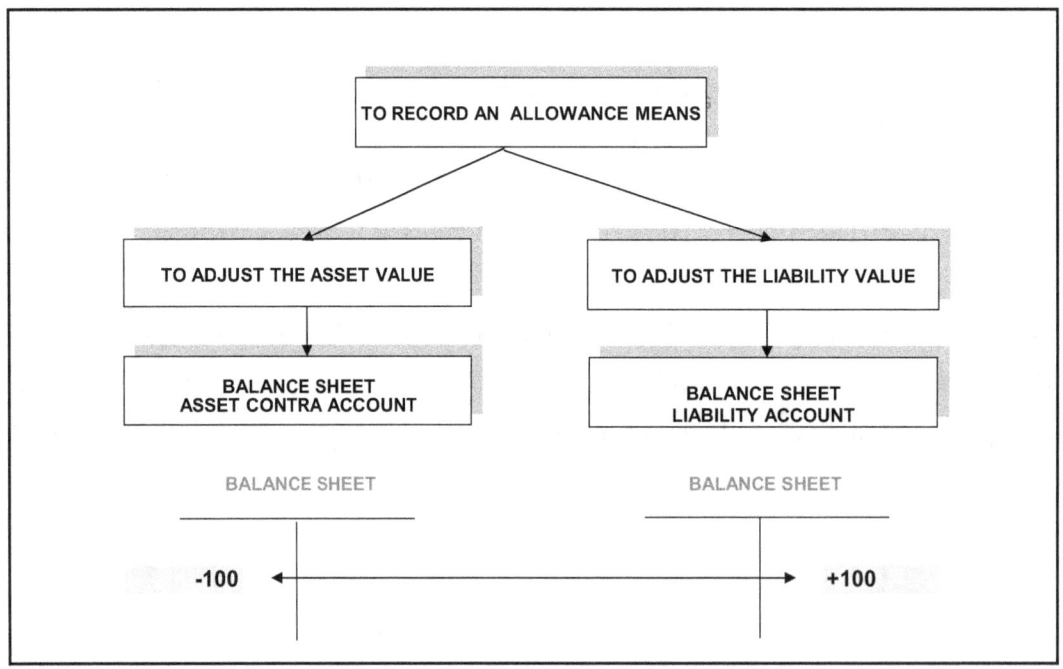

Accounting principles and process
The accounting process

36 Adjustment of revenues and expenses

According to the accrual concept, revenues and expenses are allocated to the period in which they occurred even if a bill is not yet issued or received.
Accrual accounting, more accurate, is the opposite of cash accounting for which revenues and services are recorded when they are paid for.

The portion which cannot be allocated to the period (and so not computed in profit and loss statement of the period) is recorded in the balance sheet. This procedure ensuring that transactions are recorded in the correct accounting period is called "cut-off"

We have 4 categories:

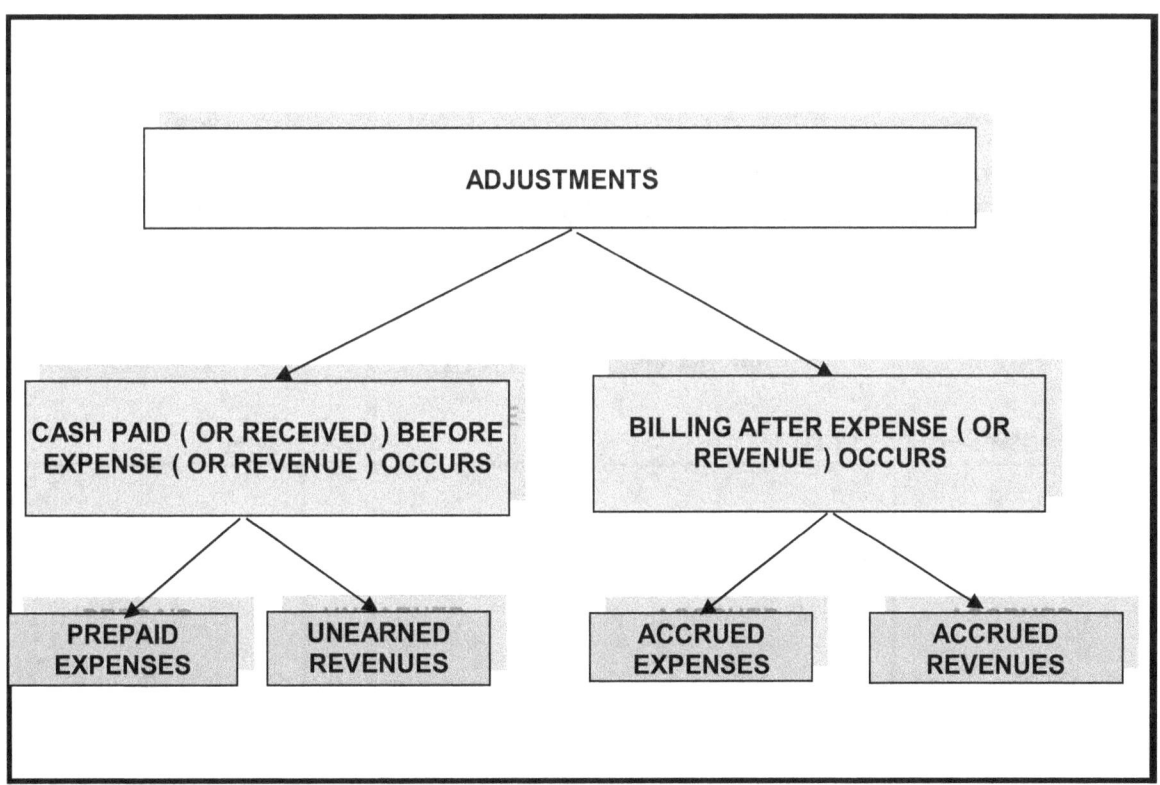

Accounting principles and process
The accounting process

- ✓ Prepaid expenses for expenses already paid in cash: they are offset from the profit and loss statement and recorded as a current asset in the balance sheet until they occur.

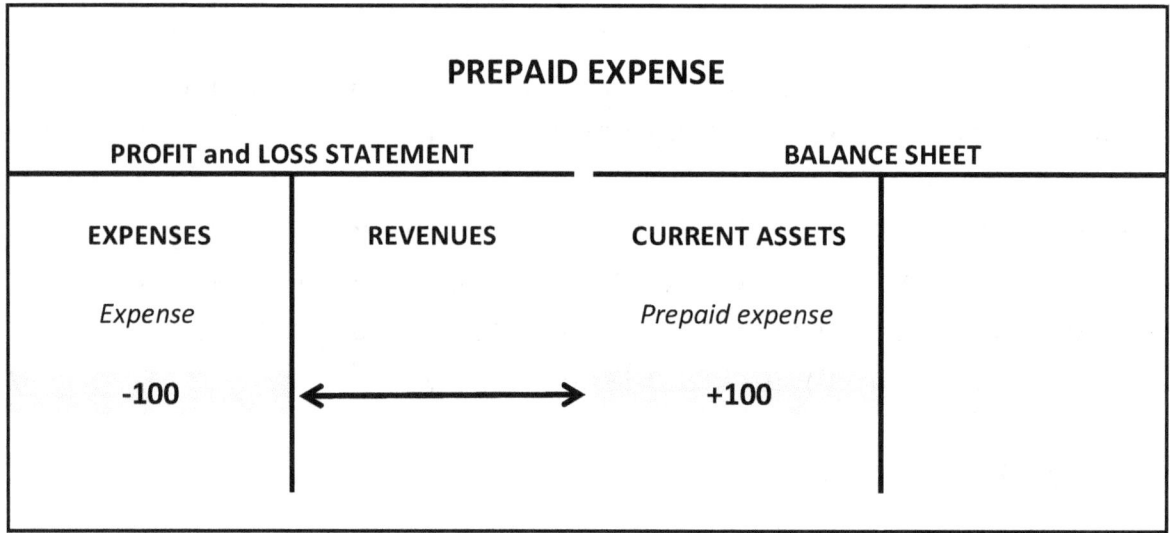

- ✓ Unearned revenues (sometimes named "deferred income) for revenues received in cash: they are offset from the profit and loss statement and recorded as a short-term liability in the balance sheet until they are earned.

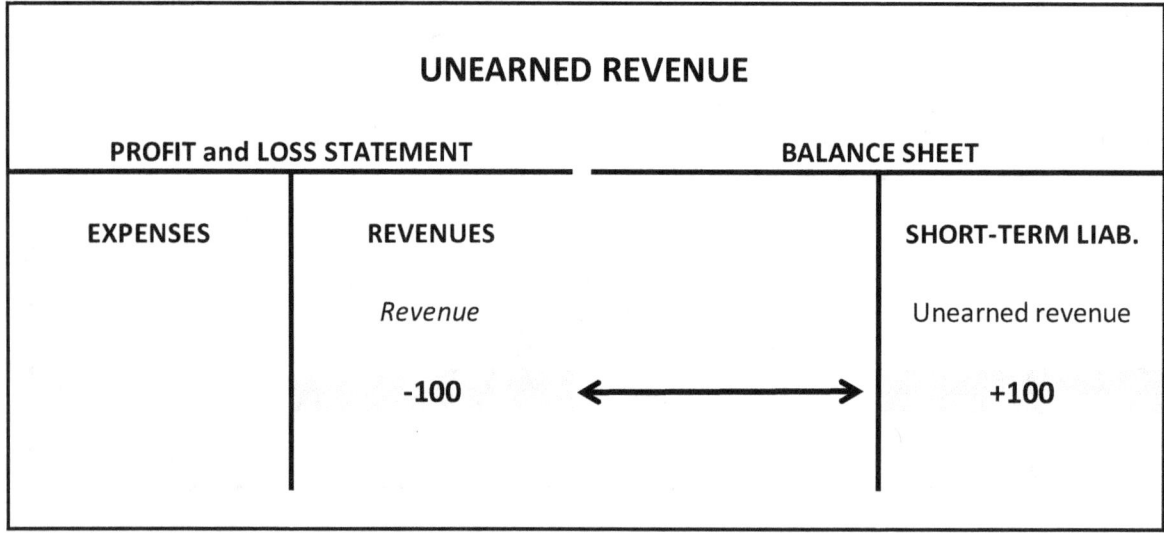

Accounting principles and process
The accounting process

- ✓ Accrued expenses for expenses occurred but not yet recorded (usually because the bill is not received): they are recorded as an expense in the profit and loss statement and as a short-term liability in the balance sheet (but not yet payable)

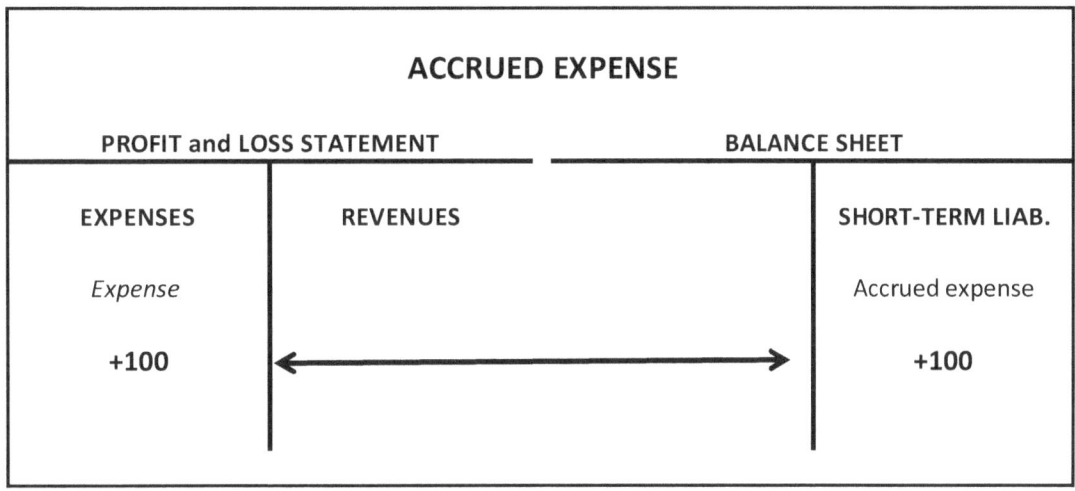

- ✓ Accrued revenues for revenues earned but not yet billed: they are recorded as a revenue in the profit and loss statement and as a current asset in the balance sheet (but not yet receivable)

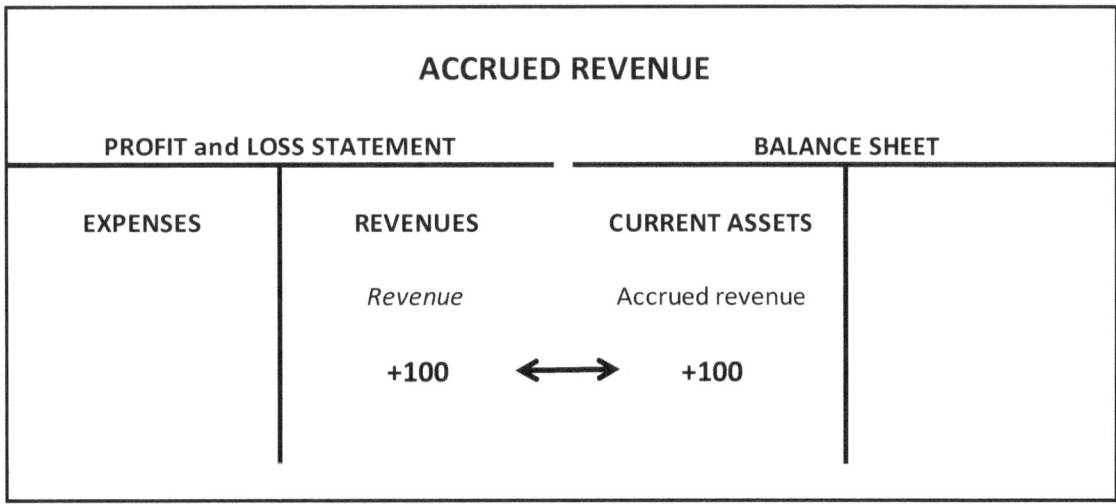

A last check of the adjusting process is made to detect possible errors through the adjusted trial balance.

Accounting principles and process
The accounting process

37 The closing process

The profit and loss statement shows the revenues and expenses of only one accounting period. Its accounts are "temporary" and should not be mixed with the accounts of the next period.
They must be closed at the end of the period in order to reset for a new accounting period.

During the closing process, the balance of each temporary account is closed and duplicated in one big account called "income summary" used to set the profit and loss statement.

The income summary is a technical tool which is not released to shareholders.

At last, the income summary is balanced by the net profit (or loss) and then closed by transferring the profit (or loss) in the balance sheet.

Towards corporate finance
Basic aspects

38 What about financial management?

Financial management practices include profitability, cash flow, long-term growth, potential risks and opportunities.

The profit and loss statement measures the activity performance and consequently its profitability.

Please refer to our book: "The profit and loss statement: 88 essentials to understand" available at AMAZON

For the other topics, the extension to the performance measurement of the company considered as a system is necessary.

Financially speaking, a company could be represented by 2 faces: invested capital and capital employed like the 2 sides of a coin.

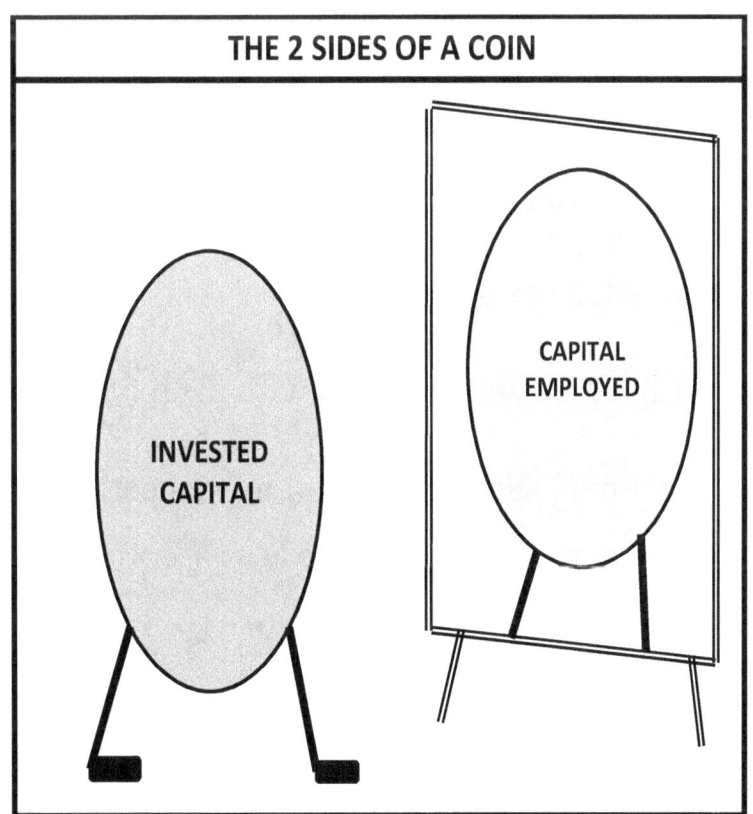

Towards corporate finance
Basic aspects

A company needs physical assets to ensure its functioning and its growth during many years: equipment, computers, offices, inventories...

These significant capital expenses are financed by cash resources raised from owners of the company (single owner or shareholders) and loaned by banks.

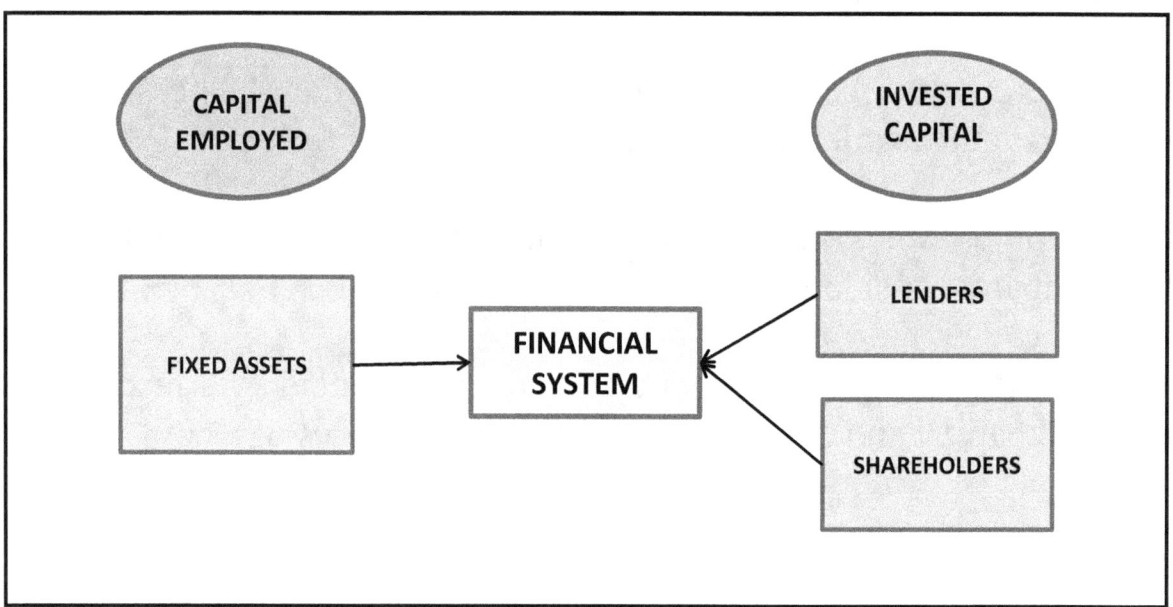

The company is a financial system with a specific structure defined by its purpose, its behaviour, its components (entities/subsystems), its processes, its risks and its growth.

Components within a system interact with each other.

The financial system is surrounded and influenced by its environment.

Towards corporate finance
Basic aspects

39 what is the impact of the activity?

A company is not only made of fixed assets invested in the past, some other means (salaries of workers and staff, lease of offices, operating expenses) are paid on a monthly basis so should be covered by the cash available.

In a B-to-B process, receivables and payables depend on payment terms which generate pending cash.

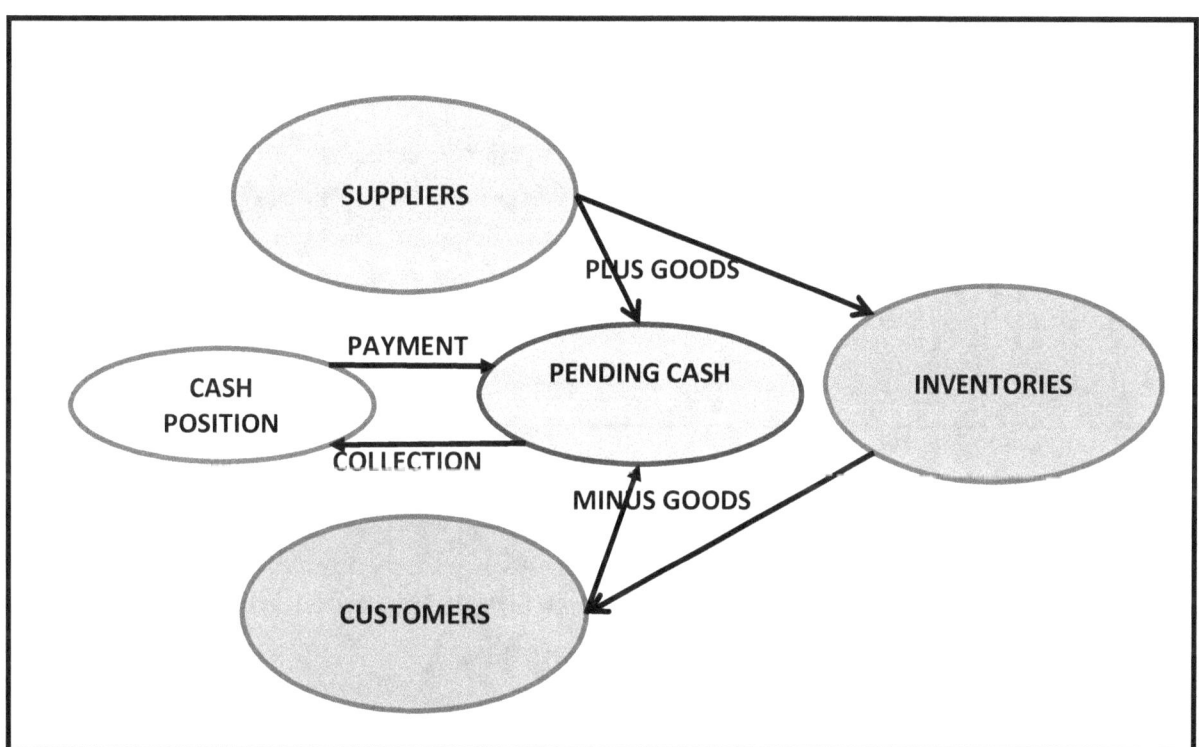

The pending cash is a sort of suction-forcing pump of the available cash position which covers not only the operational obligations but also the financial ones (interest expenses, loans repayments, dividends).

The cash surplus is reinvested in the company to create additional enterprise value (organic and/or external growth) and generate capital gains for shareholders.

Towards corporate finance
Basic aspects

So, the financial system can be showed with its components in situation.

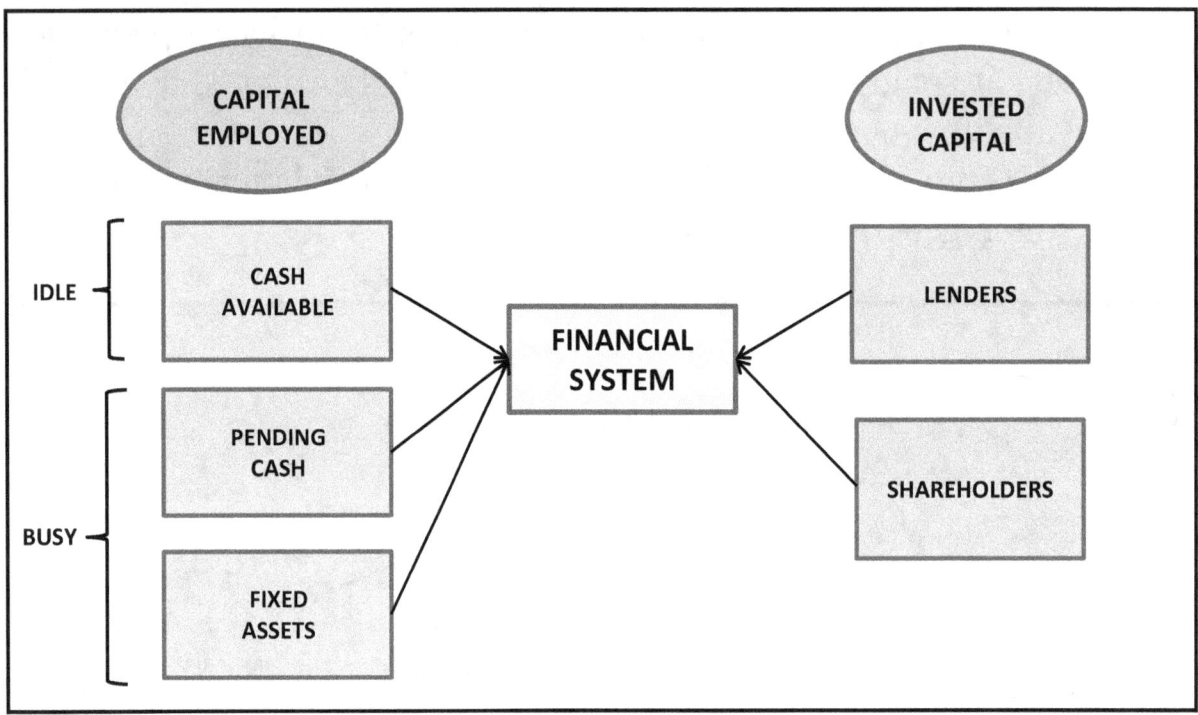

We have 2 types of capital employed:

- ✓ The busy capital generating value by the way of the company's activity (fixed assets and pending cash).

- ✓ The cash available, which is the consequence of the activity and not yet reemployed.

The busy capital employed has a return called ROCE for **R**eturn **O**n **C**apital **E**mployed.
Please refer to our book: "The profit and loss statement: 88 essentials to understand" available at AMAZON

On the other hand, the cash available has no return, or a small one if invested in marketable securities, that's why it's called: idle capital employed.

Towards corporate finance
Introducing the consequences of payment terms

40 How to calculate the pending cash?

Take an example: A company X buys a merchandise $ 40 with a down payment of $ 20 and $ 20 paid later. This merchandise is sold right away $ 100 with a down payment of $ 40.
The operation is profitable:
selling price minus purchase cost: $ 100 - $ 40 = $ 60

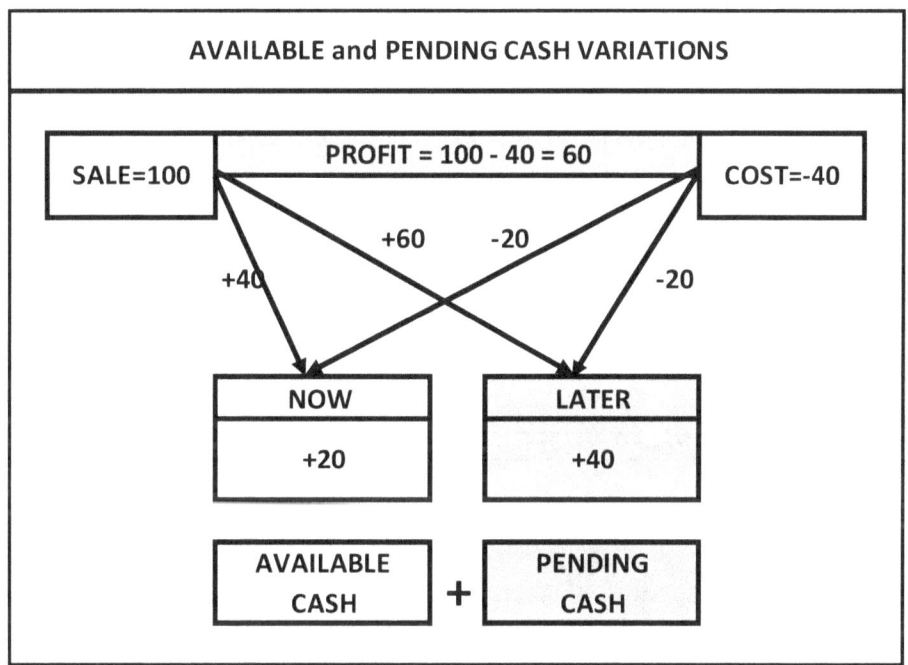

But according to the payment terms, the cash flows are:
Sale = $ 40 now + $ 60 later
Cost = $ 20 now + $ 20 later
Available cash = $ (40 – 20) = $ 20
Pending cash = $ (60 – 20) = $ 40
The profit of $ 60 is distributed into $ 20 of available cash and $ 40 of pending cash.
Of course, the cash pending will be collected later.
But, in the meantime, other sales and purchases will generate other amounts of pending cash.
.

Towards corporate finance
Introducing the working capital requirement

41 What is the meaning of working capital requirement?

Take an example: A merchandise purchased 50 is resold later 130 with a delay between the purchase and the sale. Let's analyze the fluctuations of the 2 sides of the coin: Invested capital and capital employed (busy and idle).

INVENTORY =50	GIVEN CAPITAL = 50	INVENTORY =50	CASH REQUIREMENT	PEND. CASH =130	PROFIT = 80 CASH REQUIREMENT	CASH = 80	PROFIT = 80
INITIAL BUSY CAPITAL EMPLOYED	INITIAL INVESTED CAPITAL	INITIAL BUSY CAPITAL EMPLOYED	INITIAL INVESTED CAPITAL	INITIAL BUSY CAPITAL EMPLOYED	INITIAL INVESTED CAPITAL	INITIAL BUSY CAPITAL EMPLOYED	INITIAL INVESTED CAPITAL
PURCHASE		PAYMENT		SALE		COLLECTION	
COMPANY'S IC = 0		COMPANY'S IC = 50		COMPANY'S IC = 130		COMPANY'S IC = 80	

During the purchase phase, the merchandise in inventory is paid later so the increase of busy capital employed is financed for free by the supplier. There is no additional invested capital needed from the company.

On the other hand, when paying the merchandise, cash is required meaning an additional invested capital from the company.

The sale of the merchandise leads to a pending cash of 130 financed by another additional invested capital of 80 funded by the profit of the operation.

Finally, the pending cash is transformed into cash available which allows to repay the cash requirement of 50 and let 80 of cash available to be reemployed later.

Towards corporate finance
Highlighting the working capital requirement

The invested capital coming from the company itself to finance the busy capital employed is involved during phases 2 (payment) and 3 (sale).

In phase 2, funding is provided by a loan or by available cash (already financed). In phase 3, by the profit of the operation registered in equity.

In phase 1 (purchase), the additional busy capital employed (the merchandise in inventory not yet paid) is financed by the supplier.
In phase 4 (collection), the busy capital is transformed into idle one.

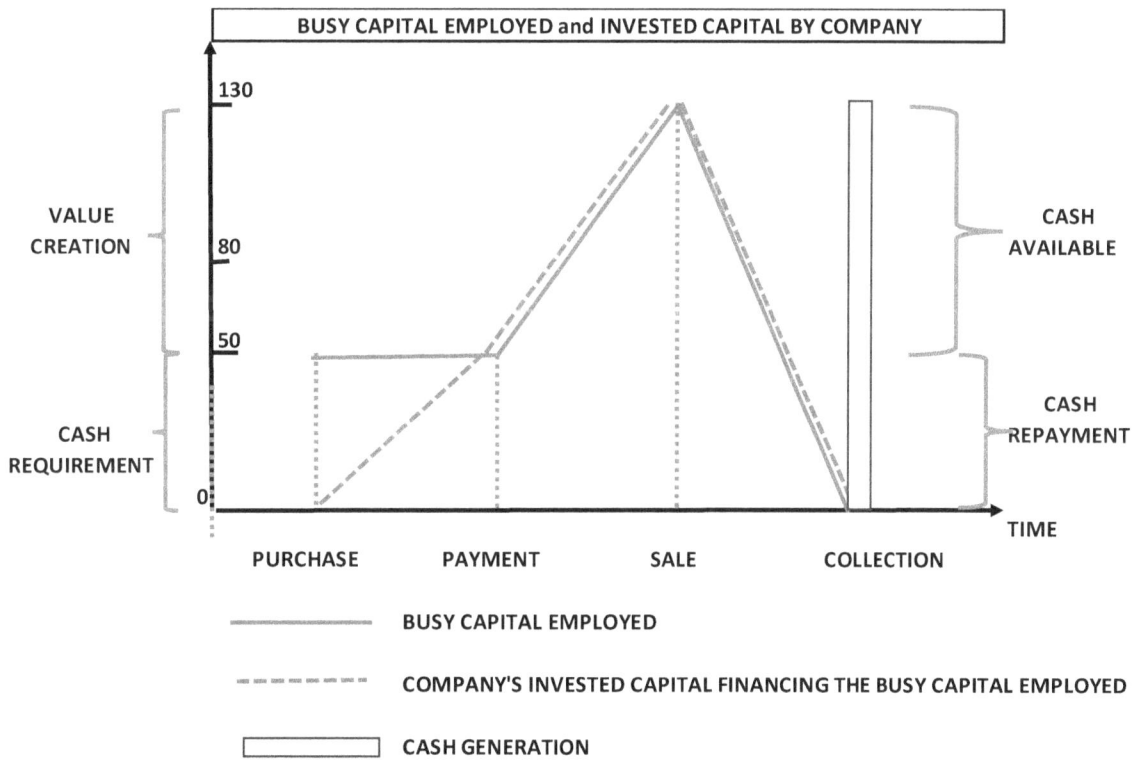

The amount of capital invested by the company itself to finance the busy capital employed is called **W**orking **C**apital **R**equirement (WCR).

Actually, we should say "invested capital required from the company to finance the busy capital employed issued by the cycle purchase-sale"

Towards corporate finance
Calculating the working capital requirement

42 How to calculate the working capital requirement?

In the example above, only one merchandise is purchased and sold. In the real life of a company, goods and services involved are at different phases of their purchase-sale cycle.

Because the working capital requirement is the busy capital employed for the purchase-sale cycle, data about fixed assets, cash position (cash, marketable securities) and company's funding (bank overdraft, note payable) are excluded.

Only are concerned, inventories, accounts receivable and prepaid expenses in current assets. Likewise, accounts payable and other payable in current liabilities.

Consequently, the working capital requirement is the balance between these current assets and current liabilities.

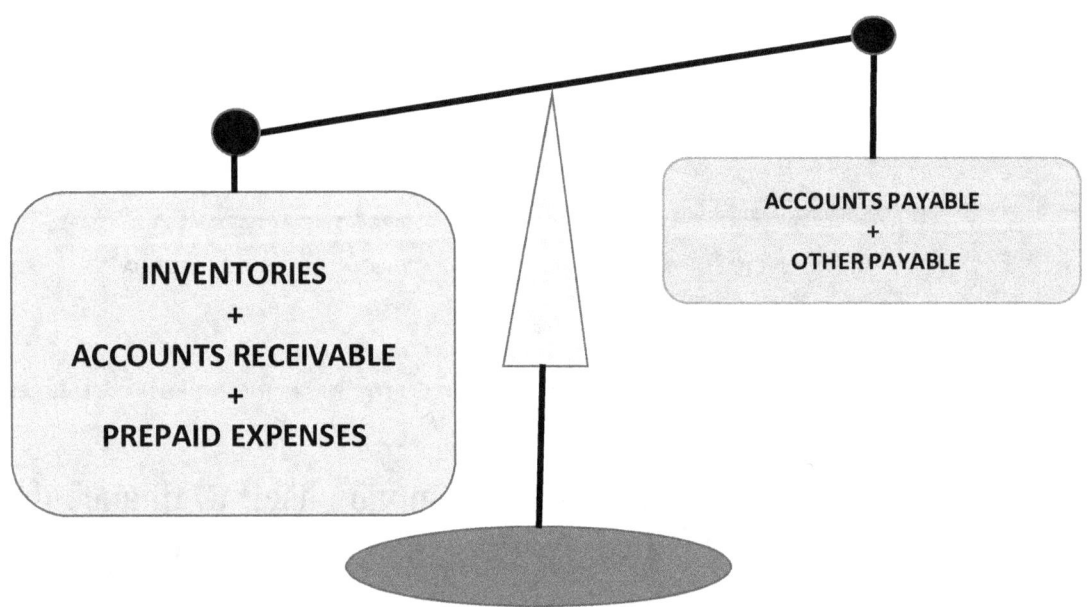

WCR = Inventories + accounts receivable + prepaid expenses
− accounts payable − other payable

48

Towards corporate finance
Calculating the working capital requirement

Using the last formula, we can check the amount of working capital requirement of the example above:

Phase 1: WCR = Inventory – account payable = 50 – 50 = 0
Phase 2: WCR = Inventory = 50
Phase 3: WCR = Account receivable = 130
Phase 4: WCR = 0

Inventories, accounts receivable and accounts payable are directly linked to the level of activity of the company over time.

Other receivable (like credit tax, deductible VAT) and other payable (like salaries and tax payable) are also linked but to a lesser extent.

The level of the working capital requirement and its oscillations with the cash position is growing with the company's activity in the space between fixed assets and invested capital.

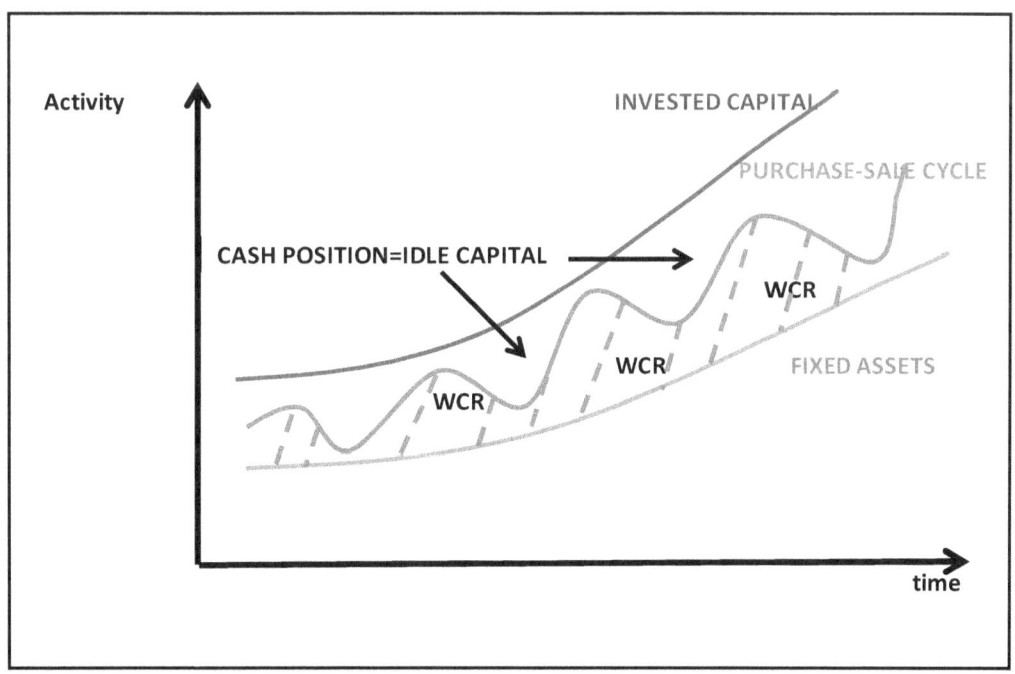

Towards corporate finance
Clues for a good practice of the capital employed

43 How to financially manage the capital employed?

According to explanations above, the pending cash is now named: working capital requirement.

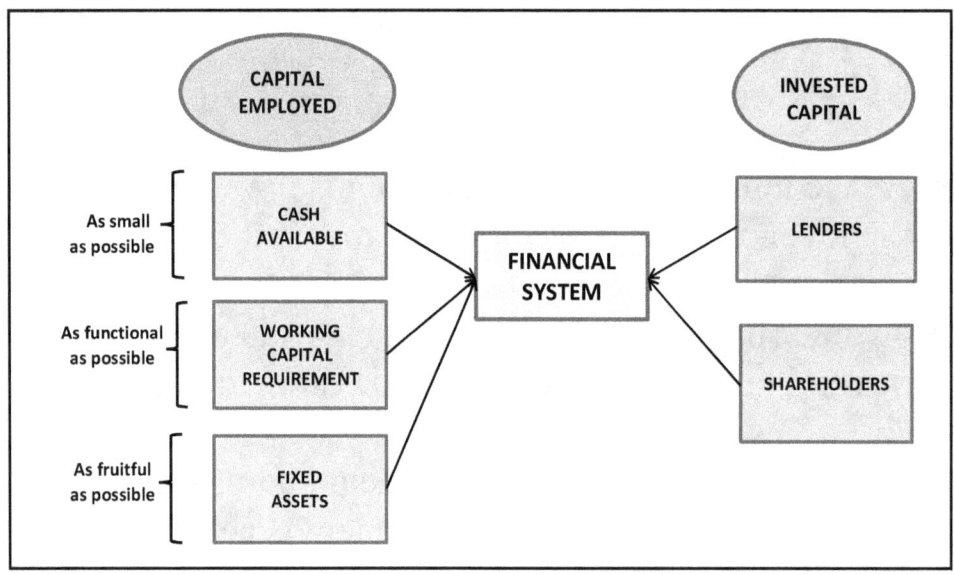

The capital employed is financed by the invested capital.
This has a cost called "**W**eighted **A**verage Cost of **C**apital" (WACC) to reward the lenders (interest rate of the loans) and the shareholders (expected gain for the risk taken in investing)

Please refer to our book: "The profit and loss statement: 88 essentials to understand" available at AMAZON

Consequently, the return on capital employed must cover and beyond the WACC which implies:

- ✓ An idle capital employed, the cash position, as small as possible.
- ✓ A busy capital employed as profitable as possible meaning a fruitful return on fixed assets and a functional management of the working capital requirement (low level of inventories, payment date to suppliers as close as possible of collection date from customers)

Towards corporate finance
The negative working capital requirement

44 could the WCR becomes negative?

The working capital requirement is negative if: inventories + accounts receivable + prepaid expenses are smaller than accounts payable + other payable

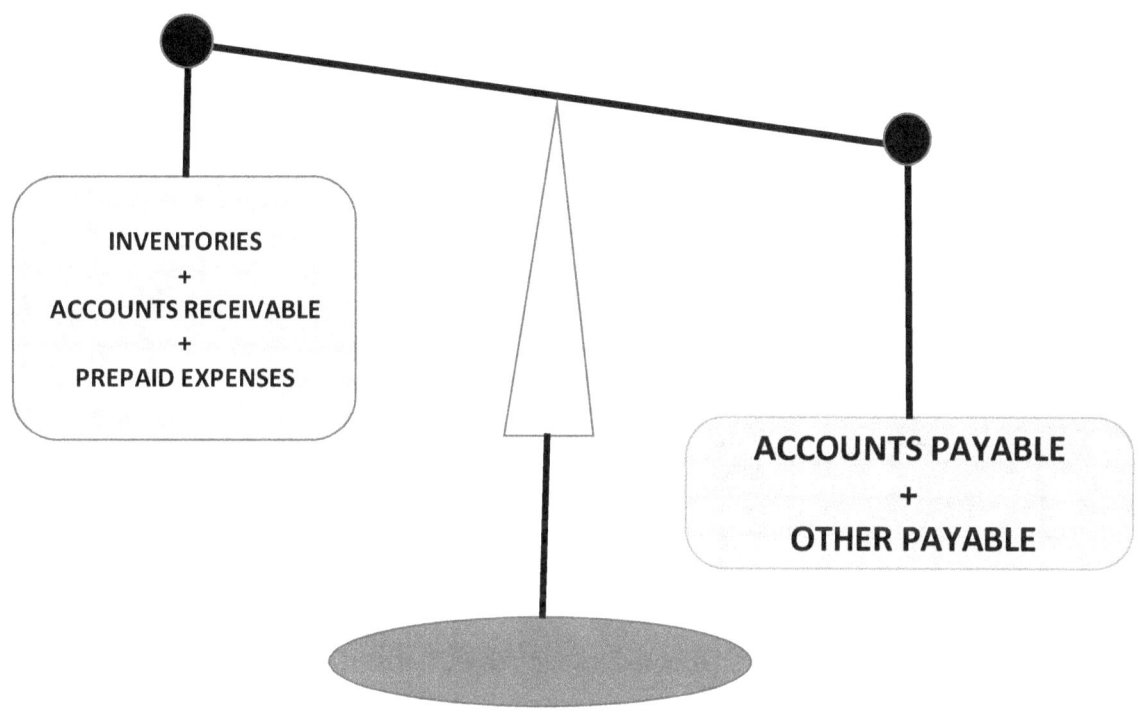

It could happen if we have a very high turnover of the inventories, a very short collection period and a long payment period to supplier (while the prepaid expenses are negligible)

The words "negative requirement" means an offer!

So, the capital employed does not require an additional invested capital from the company because the capital is offered by ... the suppliers!

We call this capital: "Opportunity capital"

Towards corporate finance
Hints to get a negative working capital requirement

45 More details about the opportunity capital

Let's have a more educational approach of the opportunity capital.

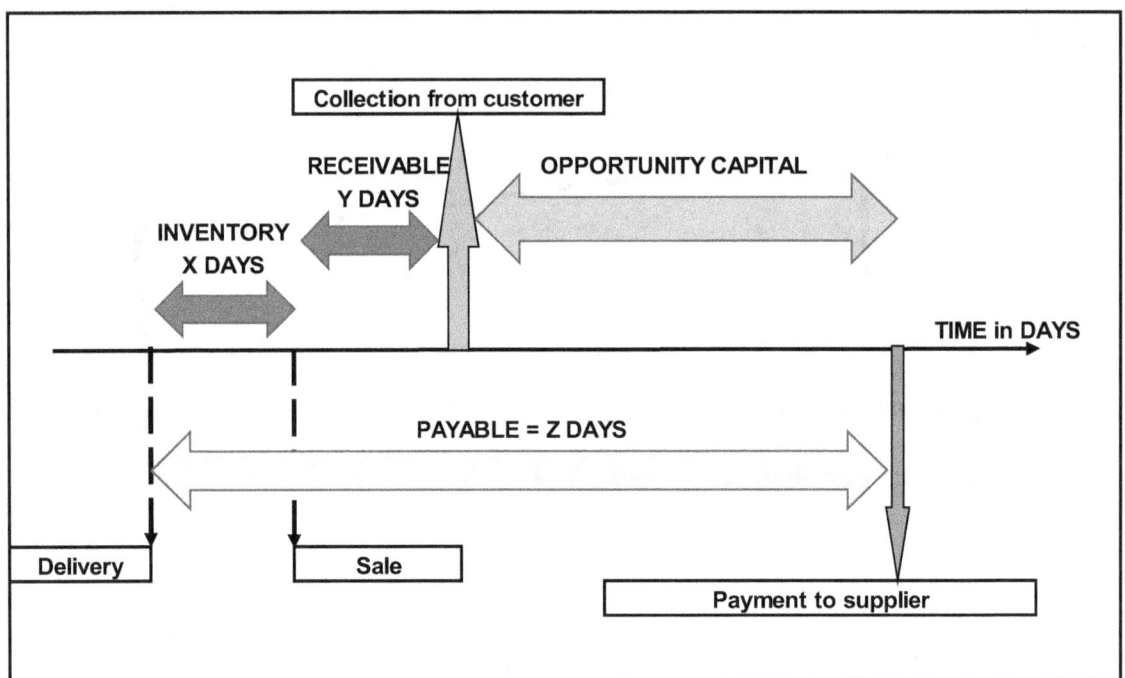

We focus on the components of the purchase-sale cycle. Inventories, accounts receivable and accounts payable.
We calculate for each of them, the average number of days of their turnover: a merchandise stays in inventory before sale during X days. It's paid by the customer on an average Y days after its sale while it's taken Z days between the delivery by the supplier and its settlement.

If $Z > X + Y$, obviously, this constantly creates a permanently renewed resource of cash conveniently financed by the suppliers.

We find this situation if a company has an efficient supply chain to lower its inventories (or no inventories at all if it provides services), makes cash sales because of a B to C business model and/or can impose long payment terms to its suppliers.
We have examples in different activities like: consignment sale, supermarkets, travel agencies and so an.

Building a financial system
From accounting vision to financial vision

46 How the financial system is related to the balance sheet?

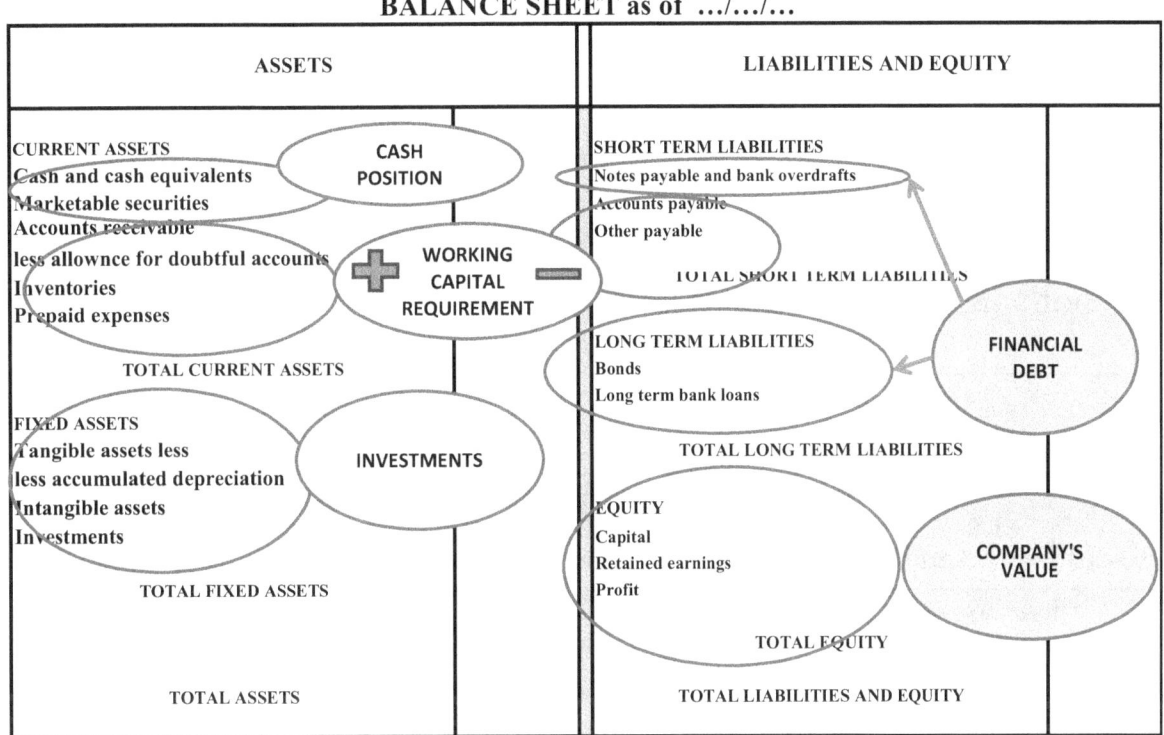

Let's take each of the balance sheet items and see how we can allocate it to one of the components of the financial system.

- ✓ Cash and cash equivalents + marketable securities constitute the cash position which is the idle capital employed

- ✓ Accounts receivable + inventories + prepaid expenses – accounts payable – other payable compute the working capital requirement seen above.

- ✓ The fixed assets (tangible, intangible and financial) are the long-term investments of the company.

The two last serve as busy capital employed.

Building a financial system
From accounting vision to financial vision

- ✓ Note payable and bank overdrafts + long-term liabilities exhibit the financial debt considered as capital invested temporarily by bankers for loans and public for bonds

- ✓ Equity is the capital invested or left (retained earnings) by shareholders after allocation of profit decided by the annual meeting

So, both are invested capital in the financial system

BALANCE SHEET	FINANCIAL SYSTEM	TYPE of CAPITAL
Cash + marketable securities	Cash position	Idle capital employed
Inventories + accounts receivable + prepaid expenses - accounts payable - other payable	Working capital requirement	Busy capital employed
Fixed assets	Investments	Busy capital employed
Note payable and bank overdrafts Long-term liabilities	Financial debt	Invested capital
Equity	Company's value	Invested capital

By definition, the balance sheet is balanced.

With the exception of 2 items (accounts payable and other payable) which are attached to the working capital requirement but with the sign minus, the financial system is balanced.
If the working capital requirement is negative, its absolute value becomes an opportunity capital showed as invested capital (by suppliers)

Thus, the items on the left of the balance sheet are in capital employed and the items on the right are in invested capital.

Building a financial system
From accounting vision to financial vision

We find again the concept of both sides of the coin seen in § 38 page 41.

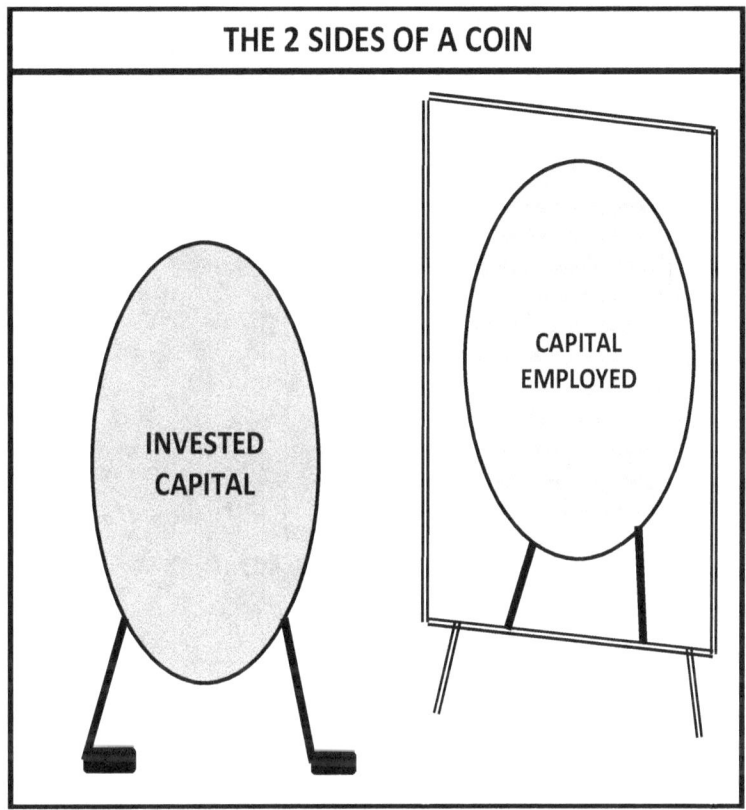

A company is analysed from the accounting point of view as a list of assets and liabilities and from the finance point of view as a list of financial resources and financial uses.

Why we speak about a financial system?

As defined by the Oxford Dictionary, a system is "a set of things working together as parts of a mechanism or an interconnecting network or a set of principles or procedures according to which something is done"

Building a financial system
From accounting vision to financial vision

47 Transforming the financial vision into a financial system.

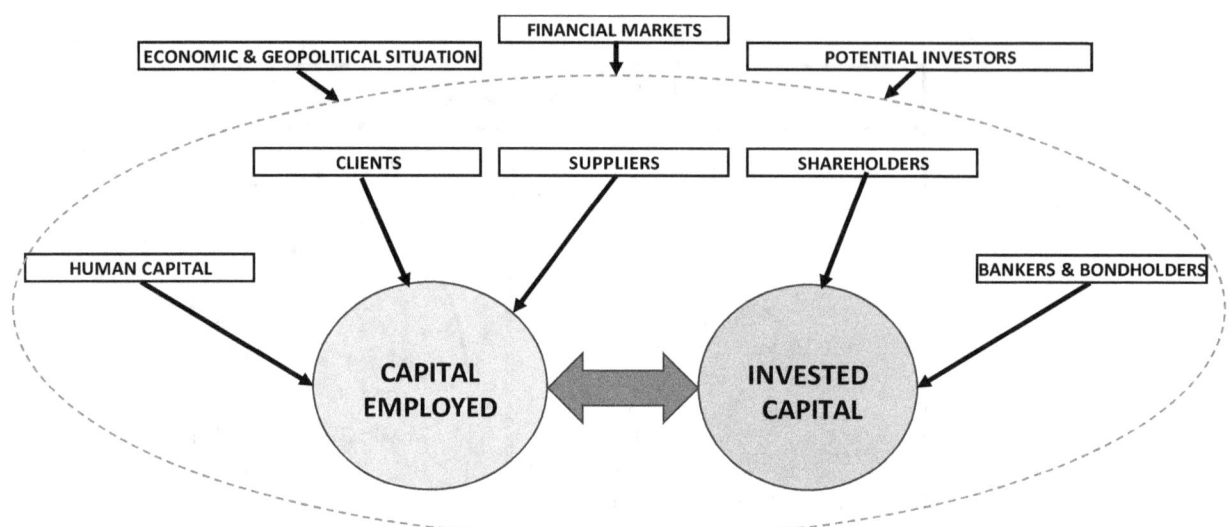

It's fruitful to address the financial vision as a whole, as a holistic system with its environment, its stakeholders and its components interacting each other.
This helps in identifying nature and volume of interactions, enhancing the value creation and overall performance, detecting potential risks and opportunities.

Having a comprehensive view, it leads to better strategic decisions, to continuous adaptations and to implementations of new solutions and technologies.

In the following pages, we will analyze the different types of models according to the weights of the different components.
We will show how some events transform their time evolution to risky situations.
Finally, we will explain the processes of value creation and cash flow generation by the components' interactions during an accounting period,

Building a financial system
From accounting vision to financial vision

48 Identification of the 5 key components of the financial system

In the financial system, the 2 sides of the coin are now side by side

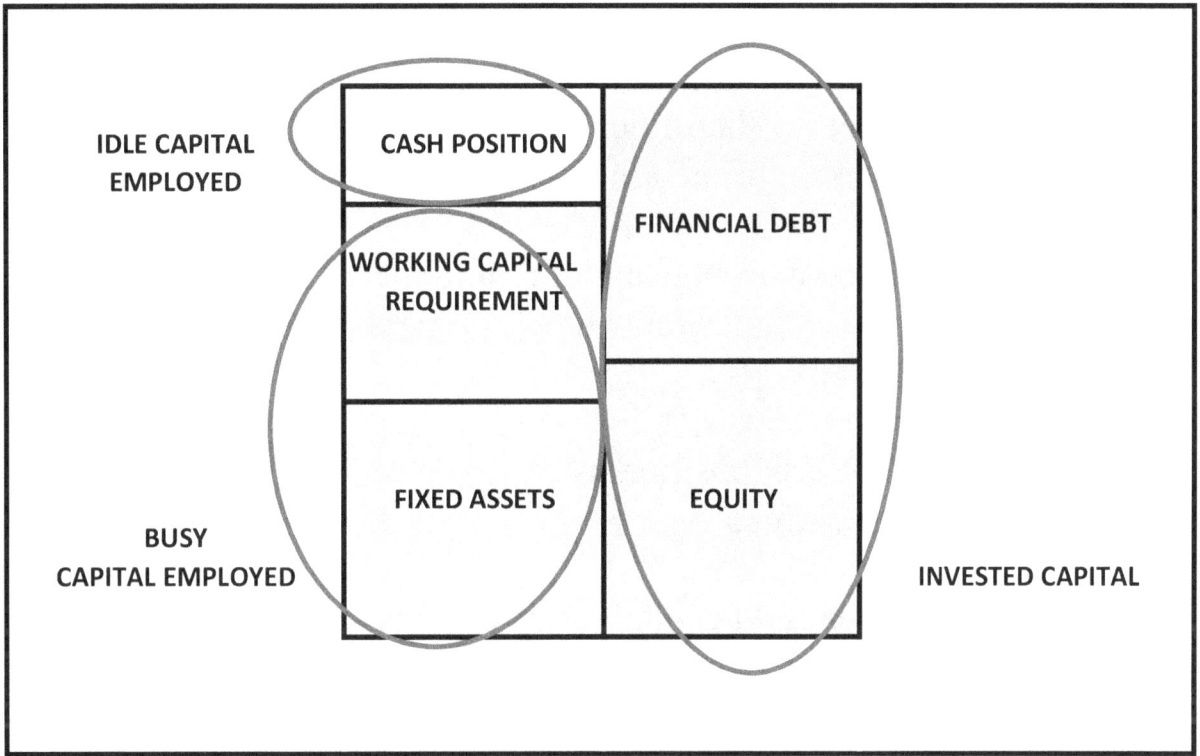

- ✓ The financial debt is the long-term and short-term financial resources invested by lenders (bankers and bondholders)

- ✓ The equity is the capital invested by shareholders or owners

- ✓ The fixed assets are employed to run the business

- ✓ The working capital requirement is like a pump that sucks and pushes back cash flows.

- ✓ The positive cash position is the idle capital already financed but not yet productively employed

Building a financial system
From accounting vision to financial vision

49 Building the financial system from the balance sheet.

- ✓ We take directly equity and fixed assets. They are identical in the balance sheet and in the financial system

- ✓ We show the financial debt by adding the long-term debt, the short-term financial liabilities (note payable and overdraft) and the current portion of the long-term debt.

- ✓ We calculate the working capital requirement as:
  Inventories + accounts receivable + prepaid expenses – accounts payable – other payable

- ✓ We define the cash position as cash and cash equivalent + marketable securities.

We check that the invested capital (equity + financial debt) and the capital employed (fixed assets + working capital requirement + cash position) are balancing. (if not, an item of the balance sheet is not correctly attached in one of the five components of the financial system)

The final structure of the financial system appears like that:
(some could be equal to zero).

On the left-hand side:
The positive cash position
The positive working capital requirement
The fixed assets

On the right-hand side:
The financial debt
The equity

Building a financial system
From accounting vision to financial vision

50 Special case of negative working capital requirement

If the working capital requirement is negative, it becomes a capital unwillingly invested by suppliers. That's why we call it opportunity capital. It should be represented in absolute value on the right-hand side of the financial system.

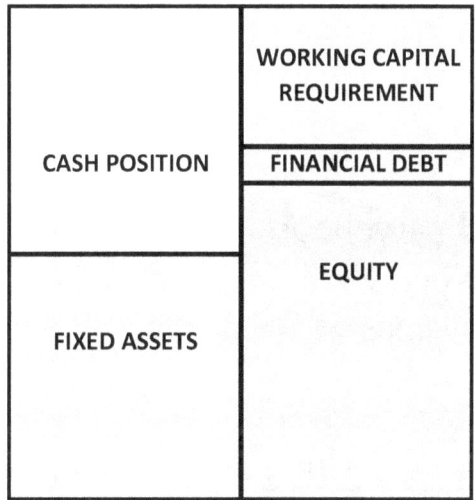

This source of financing due to important accounts payable is a short-term capital which may lead to a mismatched maturity risk seen later in § 60 page 72.

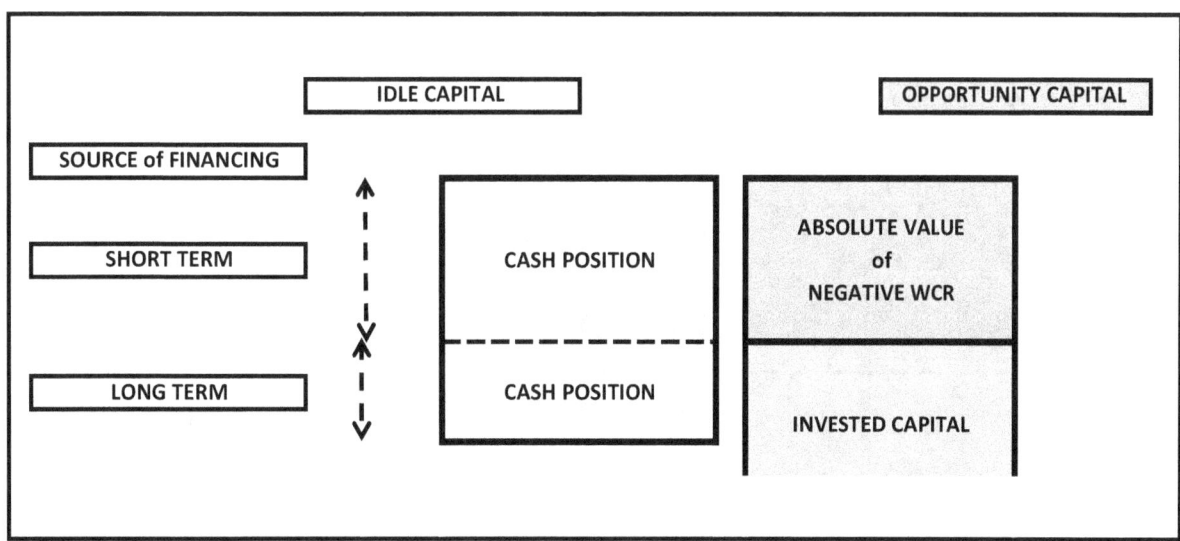

Building a financial system
Case study

51 Representation of a "common-size financial system"

The items of the financial system are presented not in absolute figures but as percentage of the total of each side.

By this way, it's possible to compare the financial systems of other companies of different size in the same sector of activity to make benchmarks and to prepare the implementation of Key Performance Indicators.

52 Case study

The balance sheet of "marvellous shoes", a US wholesale store selling to retailers, is detailed below:
The figures are in thousands of US dollars.

BALANCE SHEET as of 12/31/N in 000 of $

ASSETS				LIABILITIES AND EQUITY	
CURRENT ASSETS				**SHORT TERM LIABILITIES**	
Cash and cash equivalents			90	Notes payable and bank overdrafts	290
Marketable securities				Accounts payable	94
Accounts receivable	394			Other payable	116
less allowance for doubtful accounts	0		394		
Inventories			696	**TOTAL SHORT TERM LIABILITIES**	500
Prepaid expenses			15		
				LONG TERM LIABILITIES	
TOTAL CURRENT ASSETS			1 195	Bonds	
FIXED ASSETS				Long term bank loans	530
Tangible assets	1030				
less accumulated depreciation	329		701	**TOTAL LONG TERM LIABILITIES**	530
Intangible assets				**EQUITY**	
Investments			273	Capital	929
				Retained earnings	210
TOTAL FIXED ASSETS			974		
				TOTAL EQUITY	1 139
TOTAL ASSETS			2 169	**TOTAL LIABILITIES AND EQUITY**	2 169

Building a financial system
Case study

Review of the asset's items:

- ✓ -Some cash available in bank accounts (cash = 90)
- ✓ -An amount of 394 not yet collected from its customers (retailers) without any allowance for doubtful accounts
- ✓ -A merchandise inventory (shoes) valued at 696
- ✓ -Some prepaid expenses for 15 (rent paid in advance)
- ✓ -Tangible assets (storage warehouses) for an historical value of 1 030 and depreciated of 329 to get a net value of 701
- ✓ An investment of 273 (value of shares owned) which is a stake in a shoes manufacturer

Review of the right-hand side of the balance sheet:

- ✓ -A short-term financial debt (note payable and overdraft = 290)
- ✓ -Some accounts payable (94) due to suppliers
- ✓ -Other payable (116): due to tax administration (income tax), to shareholders (dividends), and to employees (salaries of December)
- ✓ -A long-term bank loan of 530
- ✓ -A capital of 929 (929,000 shares of a nominal value of 1 $) which is the capital invested by the shareholders at the start of the business.
- ✓ -Retained earnings for 210: the profit of the former years maintained in the company by decision of the shareholders instead of distributing as dividends. It's considered as reinvested capital.

This information is extracted from "the notes to financial statements" provided by the company.

Building a financial system
Case study

53 Case study: Building the financial system of the company

We have first to identify the five financial sections explained in § 48 page 57.

Three are directly read from the balance sheet:

- Fixed assets (**FA**) = 974
- Equity (**E**) = 1 139
- Positive cash position (**CP$^+$**) = 90

Two sections need a calculation:

- Financial debt (**FD**) = Long-term financial debt + short-term financial debt (note payable and overdraft).
  Financial debt (**FD**) = 530+290 = 820

- Working Capital Requirement (**WCR**) = inventories + accounts receivable + prepaid expenses – accounts payable – other payable

  Working Capital Requirement (**WCR**) = 696+394+15–94–116
  Working Capital Requirement (**WCR**) = 895

We notice:

- The **WCR** is positive meaning that the day-to-day business creates a pending cash.

- The company has a positive cash position (**CP$^+$=90**) but we have simultaneously a short-term financial debt of 290.

Then, we check the total of each side of the financial system.

Building a financial system
Case study

Capital employed = **CP⁺ + WCR + FA** = 90 + 895 + 974 = 1 959
Invested capital = **FD + E** = 820 + 1 139 = 1 959

The financial system is balanced.

FINANCIAL SYSTEM as of December 31st year N					
CAPITAL EMPLOYED			**INVESTED CAPITAL**		
CP+	90	4,6%	ST FD	290	14,8%
WCR	895	45,7%	LT FD	530	27,1%
FA	974	49,7%	EQUITY	1 139	58,1%
TOTAL	1 959	100,0%	**TOTAL**	1 959	100,0%

The amount of short-term financial debt represents more than half of the long-term financial debt. So, we decide to show it separately to better analyze the financial system.

```
┌─────────────────────────────────┐
│  CP+ 4,6%      │                │
│                │  ST FD 14,8 %  │
│                │                │
│                ├────────────────┤
│  WCR 45,7%     │  LT FD 27,1%   │
│                │                │
│                ├────────────────┤
│                │                │
│                │   E 58,1 %     │
│  FA 49,7 %     │                │
│                │                │
└─────────────────────────────────┘
```

Let see now how we can analyze a financial system

Financial systems' snapshot
The 8 remarkable types of financial systems

54 Financial system analysis

The systems are built from the balance sheet set at the closing date. (In most cases, the closing date is the last day of the calendar year: December 31st, but according to their business seasonality, some companies decide to choose an accounting cycle different from the calendar year).

In the following pages, we assume that the balance sheets give a standard situation of the company.

According to the proportions of the sections, we propose eight remarkable financial systems grouped in three categories in terms of risk and efficiency.

- ✓ The optimal systems
- ✓ The lazy systems
- ✓ The risky systems

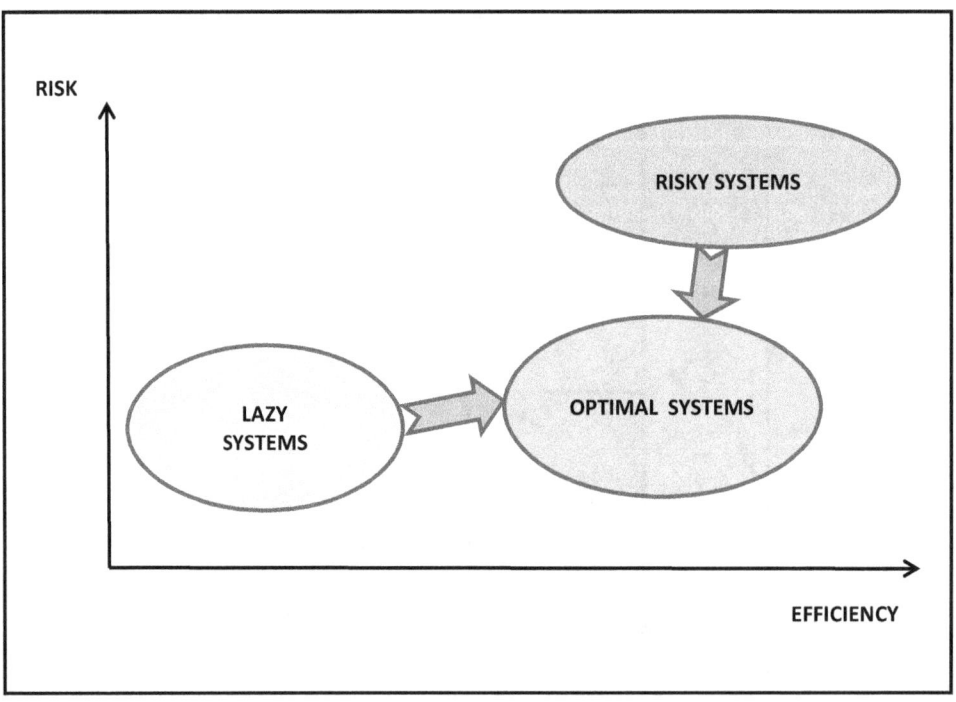

Let's start with the optimal systems (ideal/ predominant/ cash machine) supposed to have a better efficiency-risk ratio.

Financial systems' snapshot
The 8 remarkable types of financial systems

55 The ideal system

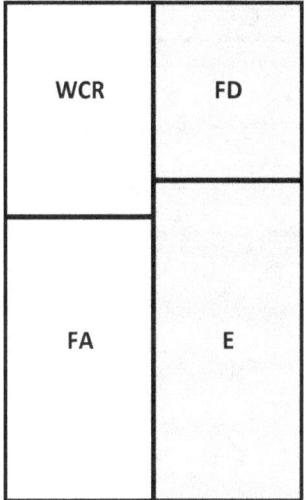

A positive cash position (**CP+**) does not generate high financial income although it is funded by the resources (**E** and **FD**) which are not for free.
Consequently, the positive cash position has to be as low as possible. In this system, named "ideal", the busy capital employed (**FA** and **WCR**) is exactly covered by the financial resources (**E** and **FD**).

This "ideal" model is not easy to realize because the working capital requirement is moving every day but some solutions are possible like:

- ✓ Implementation of a financial software to streamline processes of invoicing and payments.

- ✓ Negotiation of a cash pooling system to centralize the cash position of multiple different bank accounts.

Otherwise, the company could create an automate allocation of excess cash to short-term investments like certificates of deposit (CDs), or treasury bills. These instruments offer liquidity but generate a modest return on investment.

Financial systems' snapshot
The 8 remarkable types of financial systems

56 The predominant system

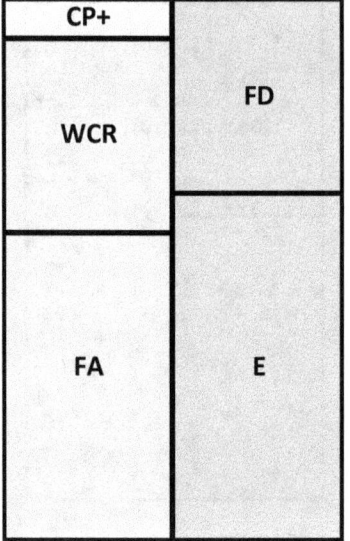

This system is the most usual.
The working capital requirement (**WCR**) is positive and fluctuating around a pivot value.

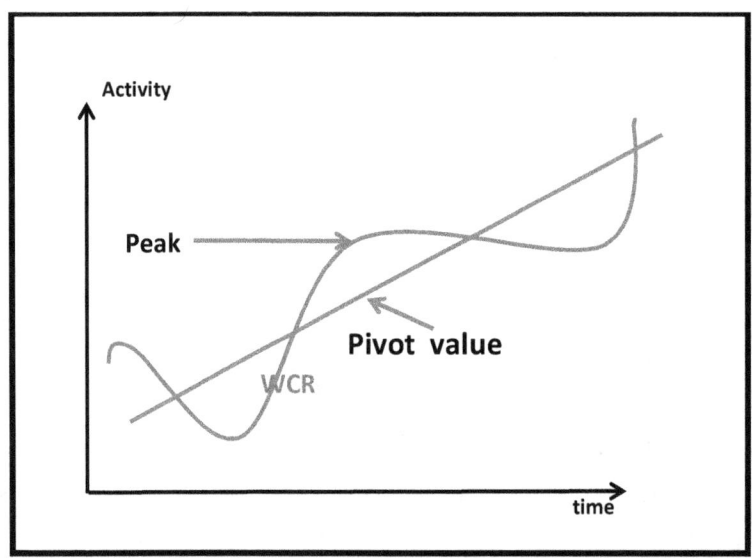

The pivot value is increasing proportionally to the company's activity.

Financial systems' snapshot
The 8 remarkable types of financial systems

Indeed, the three main components of the working capital requirement (inventories level, customers receivable and suppliers payable) are proportional to sales.

If the company's transactions are profitable, the growth of sales creates an additional profit recorded in equity and consequently an increase of the financial resources to absorb the average increase of the working capital requirement.

The permanent positive cash position (**CP+**) is used to face the current payments as seen in § 41 page 46.

57 The cash machine system

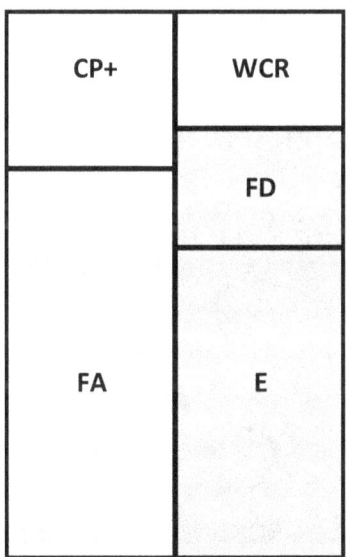

In this system, we have a negative working capital requirement (**WCR**) represented in absolute value on the right-hand side of the system.

This creates a financial resource for free called opportunity capital seen in § 50 page 59.
In case of successful business, the increase of sales will generate mechanically more and more cash.

Financial systems' snapshot
The 8 remarkable types of financial systems

But this opportunity capital is a short-term financial resource linked to the business cycle. A sudden drop of the activity could decrease the level of negative **WCR** and consequently the level of financial resources. Using this short-term resource to finance long term fixed asset could be a strategic financial mistake

The finance manager has to define the percentage of negative **WCR** and so the amount of cash possibly invested in fixed assets without too high risk. The remaining amount of cash can be invested in short-term deposits or low risky securities (marketable securities) to get some additional revenues.

There is another profitable and safer short-term possibility to use the excess of net cash position by paying earlier some suppliers in exchange of financial discounts.
(Paying a supplier 1 month earlier in exchange of a discount of 2 % is equivalent to invest this money at a rate of 24 % on a yearly basis!!).

Let's analyse now two other systems with a very excessive positive cash position.

- ✓ The fat cash system
- ✓ The cash overflow system

On the graph efficiency-risk seen above, these systems with a high idle capital employed generating a low yield but have a lower risk by securing the solvency of the long-term debt and the illiquidity of unexpected expenses.

Financial systems' snapshot
The 8 remarkable types of financial systems

58 The fat cash system

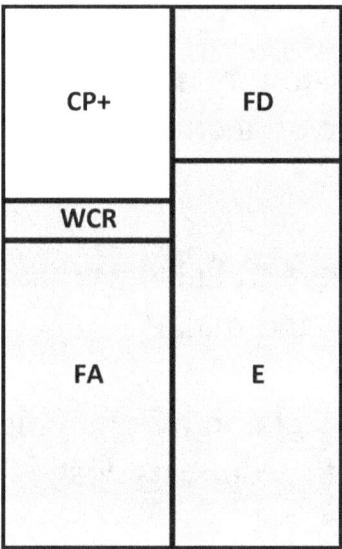

In this system the positive cash position (**CP+**) is very high without coming from a negative **WCR**. This permanent situation is comfortable but requires management reactions.

The cause is a constant high performance producing cash flows which are idly employed.

Because the financial resources have a cost called "**W**eighted **A**verage **C**ost of **C**apital" (**WACC**), these cash flows in excess must be re-employed to avoid a drop of the financial performance.

Please refer to our book: "The profit and loss statement: 88 essentials to understand" available at AMAZON.

So, it's crucial to avoid a waste of resources by transforming a too high positive **CP+** with a limited return into profitable operating assets.

Financial systems' snapshot
The 8 remarkable types of financial systems

For example, the management could consider:

- ✓ A strategic decision by diversifying into a new business line.

- ✓ An operational decision by investing in efficient equipment, buying a brand name or acquiring a competitor to make synergies

The financial management could also use the excess of cash to repay a portion of invested capital and make:

- ✓ A tactical financial decision by repaying a portion of the financial debt (**FD**) to reduce its cost.

- ✓ A strategic financial decision by increasing the dividend payout which could lead to a rise of the shares' market price and potential capital gains for shareholders.

- ✓ A "buy back" especially if the company is publicly listed.
  It consists in the repurchase of a portion of the capital.
  This method will be developed below in § 60 page 72.

Financial systems' snapshot
The 8 remarkable types of financial systems

59 The cash overflow system

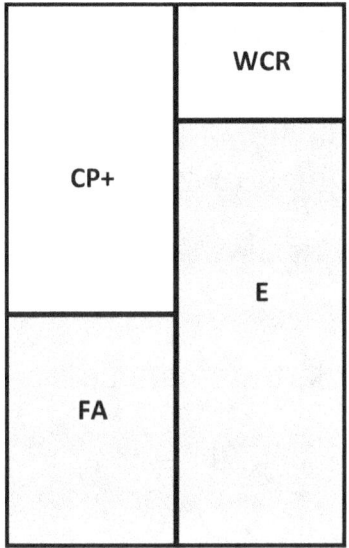

This system is a hypertrophic mix of the cash machine system (§ 57 page 67) and the fat cash system (§ 58 page 69)

The company is very profitable and simultaneously has a negative working capital requirement (**WCR**): the high performance and the sales growth generate together a permanent high cash flow.

The company has already used cash to repay the financial debt (**FD**) and we suppose that the fixed assets are diversified and efficient.

This situation is supposed to be sustainable over time.

The ultimate possibility is the "shares buy back".

This technique refers to the repurchasing by a company of its outstanding shares to delete them and to reduce the number available on the open market.

Financial systems' snapshot
The 8 remarkable types of financial systems

60 What is the mechanism of a "buy back"

A company uses the excess of cash to propose to their shareholders to buy back a portion of its own shares at the price in the marketplace.

The shares acquired by the company from the shareholders accepting the proposal are deleted which reduces the level of equity.

On the other hand, the busy capital employed remains constant.

After a successful buy back, the financial system has this "ideal" aspect:

CP+	WCR
FA	E

Two effects:

- ✓ For the company and its remaining shareholders, the return on the capital employed in fixed assets (**FA**) is allocated to fewer shareholders inflating earnings per share and consequently the market price of the share.

- ✓ For the former shareholders having decided to sell their shares to the company, the money back allows them to invest in other companies and diversify their portfolio.

Financial systems' snapshot
The 8 remarkable types of financial systems

Continuing the description of the systems, we have three causes of risk impacting the financial systems.

- ✓ An illiquidity risk caused by a permanently high short-term borrowing

- ✓ An insolvency risk due to a too ratio financial debt/equity

- ✓ A mismatch risk between the maturities of invested and employed capital.

61 The cash shortage system

WCR	ST FD
	FD
FA	E

In the cash shortage system, the positive cash position (**CP+**) is missing and the company uses a short-term financial debt (note payable and overdraft) (**ST FD**) to face its obligations.

This short-term financial debt while it could be suddenly questioned by the bank leading to an illiquidity situation.

As usual, solutions are operational and/or financial:

Financial systems' snapshot
The 8 remarkable types of financial systems

- ✓ An operational solution: speeding the transformation of pending cash into available cash by reducing the working capital requirement (**WCR**). This goes through improving the inventories turnover, collecting bills earlier even by financial discount or trying to pay the suppliers later.

- ✓ A tactical financial solution: to negotiate with the bankers by transforming the overdraft and the short-term financial debt into a long-term financial debt.

62 Insolvency risk system

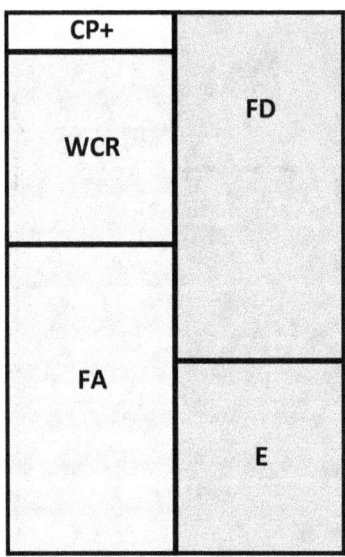

If liquidity refers to the company's ability to meet its short-term obligations (short-term financial debt), solvency represents the company's ability to meet its long-term obligations.

This can occur if the entity's liabilities exceed its assets, struggling operations in the long run and leading to financial distress and potential bankruptcy.

Financial systems' snapshot
The 8 remarkable types of financial systems

Three aspects are useful to analyse:

- ✓ The cost of the interest expenses (the interest rate is in relation with the level of the debt and the risk of the borrower) which reduces the performance

- ✓ The repayment of the financial debt (**FD**) which deteriorates the free cash flow.

- ✓ The high level of the financial debt (**FD**) in comparison with the level of equity (**E**) to highlight the stake of bankers and shareholders in the allocation of invested capital.

Ratios like interest coverage, debt coverage and debt-to-equity are relevant to assess the solvency risk.

The possible solutions are:

- ✓ The decrease of the working capital requirement (**WCR**) as seen above for the cash shortage system

- ✓ The sale of non-strategic fixed assets.

- ✓ The increase of equity (**E**) by issue of new shares of capital
  This solution reduces the yearly interest expenses and the repayment cash outflow. In exchange, the company may be required to pay more dividends.
  It also increases the **W**eighted **A**verage **C**ost of **C**apital (**WACC**) with consequences for the performance.

Please refer to our book: "The profit and loss statement: 88 essentials to understand" available at AMAZON.

Financial systems' snapshot
The 8 remarkable types of financial systems

- ✓ The resale of strategic assets backed by a leasing contract with an investment bank. This purchases and pays cash the company's asset (e.g. the head office). The company continues to use its asset leased asset and get it back for free at the maturity of the contract.

This arrangement called leaseback or sale-leaseback allows to clean-up a distressed situation and even to invest in high-performing strategic assets.

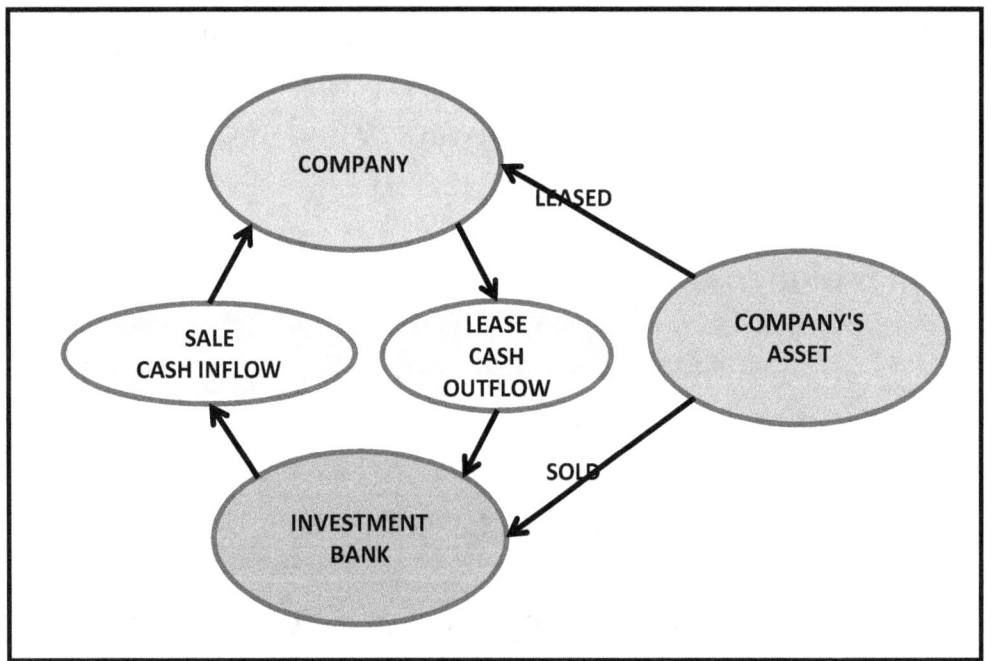

This solution has some aside advantages like:

- ✓ The lease payments are often tax-deductible unlike capital repayments
- ✓ The operational stability of assets is kept
- ✓ The asset and the associated debt are off the balance sheet which improves the financial ratios.

Financial systems' snapshot
The 8 remarkable types of financial systems

63 Mismatched maturities system

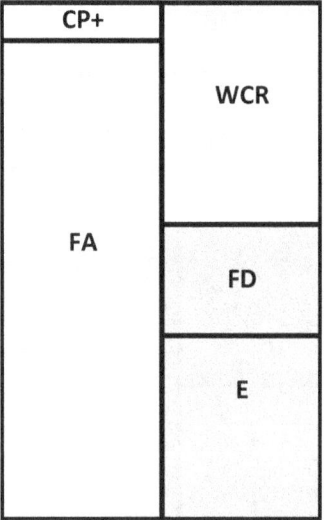

In this case, the company's business model creates a negative working capital requirement (**WCR**) like in a cash machine system (see § 57 page 67).
But cash flow generated by this situation has been already mainly absorbed in invested fixed assets (**FA**).
This opportunity capital with a short-term maturity (linked to purchase-sale cycle) is used to finance fixed assets (**FA**) with a long-term maturity.

Any drop of sales (recession, marketing mistake, management mistake) will decrease the negative working capital requirement (**WCR**) and delete the remaining positive cash position.

The possible solutions are:

- ✓ Boosting the sales through advertising and seller bonuses to make the working capital requirement (**WCR**) more negative and re-establish a positive cash position.

- ✓ Arranging a leaseback contract as seen above to lighten the weights of fixed assets (**FA**)

Financial systems' snapshot
The 8 remarkable types of financial systems

64 Interpreting the system seen in the study case

```
| CP+ 4,6%    |              |
|             | ST FD 14,8 % |
|             |              |
| WCR 45,7%   | LT FD 27,1%  |
|             |              |
|             |              |
|             | E 58,1 %     |
| FA 49,7 %   |              |
```

The analysis is based on 3 steps: observation, diagnosis, solution

let's first notice the proportion of every section.

- ✓ The equity (**E**) at 58,1 % covers the fixed assets (**FA**) for 49,7 %

- ✓ The long-term financial debt (**LT FD**) at 27,1 % is twice smaller than equity (**E**) which minimizes the solvency risk

- ✓ The working capital requirement (**WCR**) of 45,7 % is at around the same level than the fixed assets (**FA**) for 49,7 %

- ✓ The short-term financial debt (**ST FD**) with 14,8 % represents half of the long-term financial debt (**LT FD**)

Financial systems' snapshot
The 8 remarkable types of financial systems

Looking at the proportion of the short-term financial debt compared to the positive cash position, we recognize easily the cash shortage model seen in § 61page73.

We don't have the financial systems of the former periods to explain why the company has arrived to such a situation with a lack of cash.

Let's propose a diagnosis:

We focus on the size of the working capital requirement especially by comparison with the fixed assets:

Is it a temporary situation linked to a seasonal activity?
Is it a too fast growth of the sales implying an increase of the working capital requirement (See § 68 page 83)
Is it a decline in business activity leading to an exceptional increase of the inventories? (See § 67 page 81)
Is it a lazy management of the working capital requirement?
That's why, it's important to make a benchmark study to compare the working capital requirement indicators of the competitors in the same business sector.

How to solve this risky situation?

- ✓ An operational solution: lowering the working capital requirement (improving the supply chain or collecting bills earlier even with financial discount). Sometimes, performance can be sacrificed in favour of a higher liquidity.

- ✓ A financial solution: negotiation with the bankers to transform the short-term financial debt into long-term one (the solvency risk is moderate)

Financial system's evolution over time
How risky situations arise?

65 The financial systems, analyzed above, are generated from balance sheets which are pictures of the situation at the closing date.

An evolutive vision of the financial system, showing the changes of invested capital and capital employed in terms of activity and time, allows to react before the occurrence of a proven risk.

A constant financial strategy for dividends and funding will increase the invested capital as a function of generated profit.
A constant operating strategy for the management of inventories, receivable and payable will increase the busy capital employed according to sales' growth and new investments.

The positive cash position is moving anti symmetrically with the working capital requirement according to the purchase-sale cycle.
It should be kept optimally between 2 reefs: a waste of financial resources with a drop of the performance if too positive or an excessive use of short-term financial debt with a risk of bankruptcy if missing.

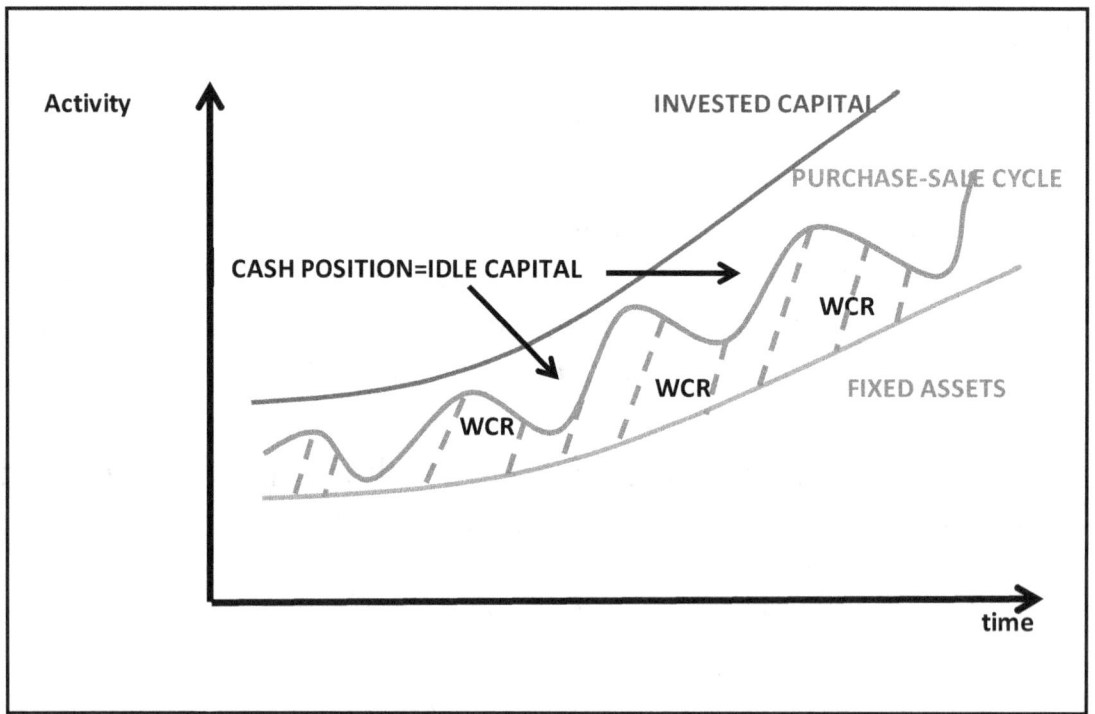

Financial system's evolution over time
How risky situations arise?

66 Need of synchronization

The synchronization between performance (generated profit) and growth (sales and investments) is necessary to avoid the lack of cash and so the bankruptcy.

So invested capital and busy capital employed should increase more or less at the same pace with an invested capital higher than a busy capital employed to keep a mattress of cash (**CP+**) ready to face the current expenses.

But we have situations of asynchronization leading to a lack of cash. Let us focus on 4 stories but you can imagine others.

In the 2 first, the busy capital employed is growing faster than the invested capital.

In the 2 last cases, the invested capital is dropping.

To make the graphs above clearer, the variations of the working capital requirement in the busy capital employed are smoothed.

67 The decline in business activity or economic recession

It looks obvious that a decline in the business activity could create a cash problem.

Economic recession, poor adaptation of products to market, technological changes, management mistakes, heavy processes, ineffective investments may cause stagnant sales.

Consequently, the inventories turnover drops, the proposed terms of payment are longer to avoid missing sales and the suppliers are greedy to be paid earlier

Financial system's evolution over time
How risky situations arise?

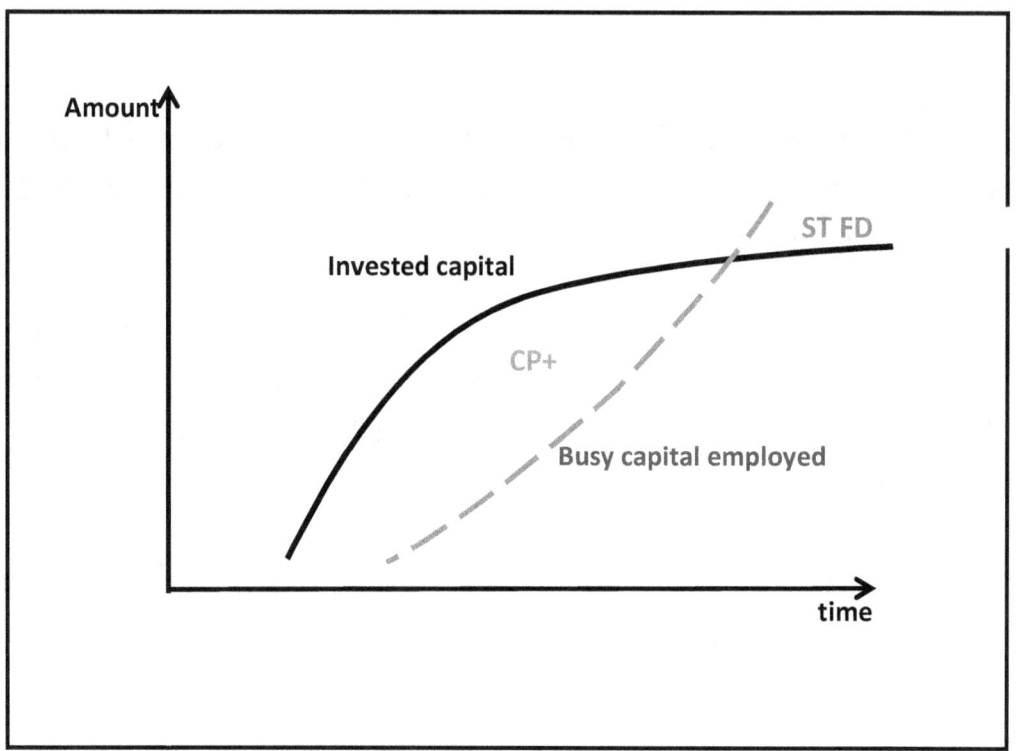

The rising of pending cash increases the busy capital employed while the invested capital is stagnant because of a poor performance. The positive cash position (**CP+**) disappears and is transformed into a short-term financial debt (**ST FD**)

We can even notice a chisel effect if a loss appears because a smaller contribution (caused by a smaller volume of sales) is less able to cover the fixed costs.

The solution is to adapt the invested capital to the new level of busy capital employed.
Borrowing money from banks is not very easy during a slump period. The cure could come from confident shareholders ready to increase their stake.
Otherwise, the company must consider a decrease of the busy capital employed by selling non-strategic assets.

Financial system's evolution over time
How risky situations arise?

68 too fast growth

In this case, strange and surprising, a company has cash problems because its business is too successful.

The increase of profitability does not match to the sales growth.

We often find this situation in start-ups having a low or even negative profitability as sales explode.

The invested capital is growing according to the performance of the company, but at the same time, the sales are booming thanks to successful products or services. The busy capital employed is rocketing by the increase of the working capital requirement and the new investments. Consequently, the mattress of idle capital employed (**CP+**) is transformed into a lack of cash financed by a short-term financial debt (**ST FD**).

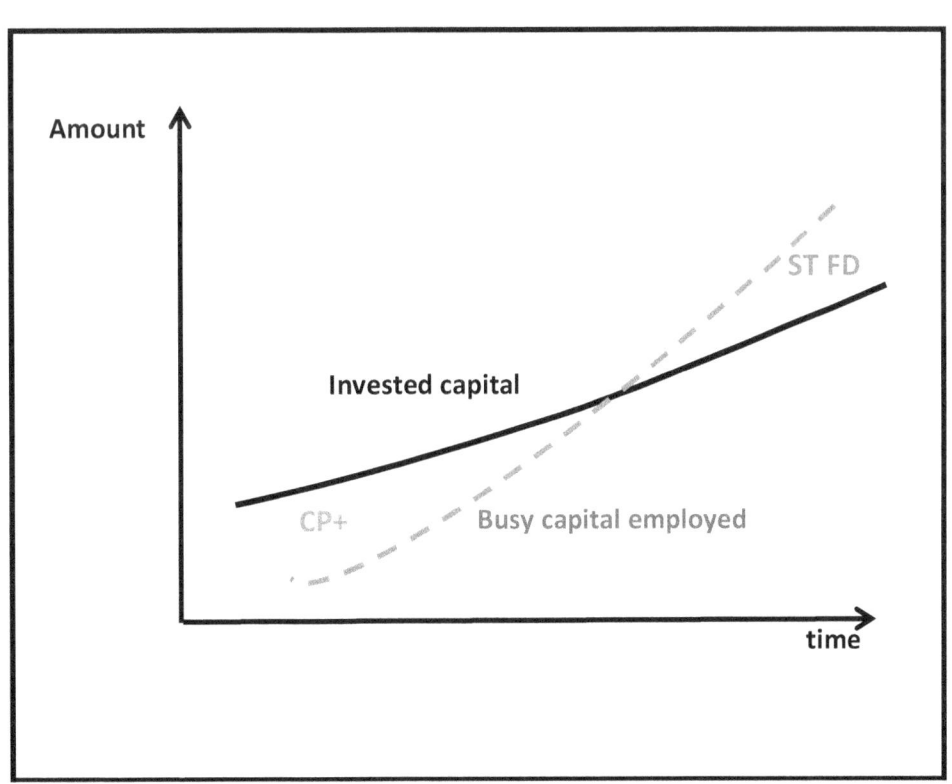

Financial system's evolution over time
How risky situations arise?

The solution is not obviously to slow down the growth but to raise new funds to increase the invested capital.

We have 2 possible solutions:

- ✓ To increase the long-term financial debt so to borrow money from the banks
- ✓ To increase the equity by raising funds from shareholders

The best solution depends on the company's relationship its shareholders and lenders.
Usually, banks consider that start-ups are too risky to lend them some money. The only opportunity is to increase their equity.
If the owners are young and not rich, the solution goes through a call to "business angels". They are wealthy individuals (sometimes formerly successful owners of start-up) who provide capital and support to a start-up in exchange of convertible debt or ownership equity.

69 Cumulated losses during several accounting cycles

Sometimes, a well-established company in its market and keen to maintain its position get during few years a non-profitable situation even with positive cash flows leading to a decrease of the equity in the invested capital.

Consequently, the invested capital will not be able to cover the busy capital employed.

To avoid overdraft and short-term financial debt (**ST FD**) and start again on new bases, the company undertakes a recapitalization operation.

Financial system's evolution over time
How risky situations arise?

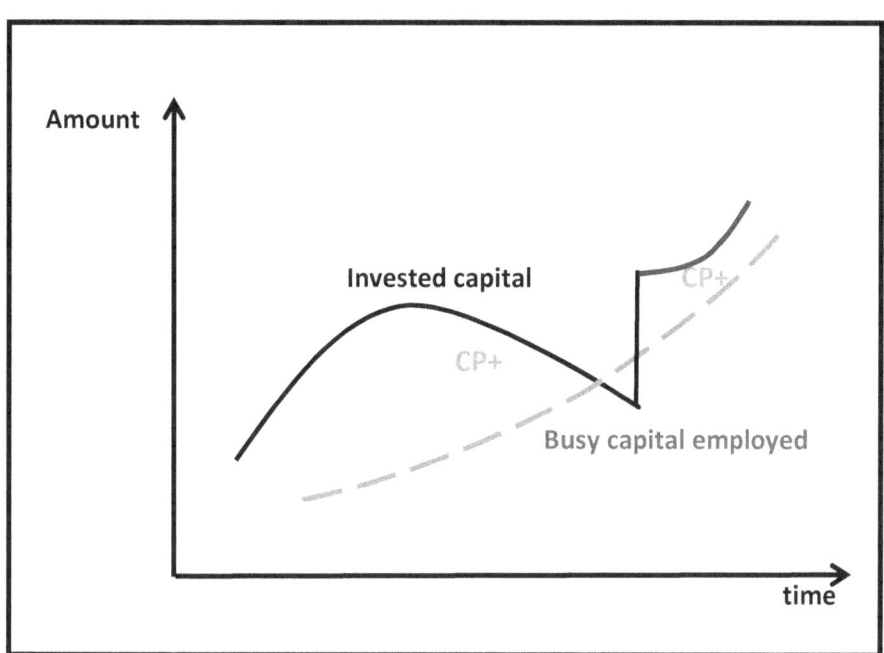

This process involves issuing new shares to raise additional funds, which can then be used to offset the accumulated losses and recreate an invested capital higher than the busy capital employed.

70 Mismatch financial mistake

This is a story of a company with a negative working capital requirement. As we have seen in § 63 page 77, comforted by a high permanent cash position, it has used its opportunity capital to finance long-term fixed assets despite a mismatched maturity risk.

Unluckily, the Covid crisis in 2019 has reduced and even deleted the opportunity capital following the change of inventories turnover and payment terms.

So, the missing invested capital has to be replaced by a bank loan or a higher stake of shareholders.

In some countries like in France, the government has proposed state-guaranteed loans waiting for a return to better days.

Financial system's evolution over time
How risky situations arise?

But the recourse to shareholders through a capital increase is the best long-term solution to allow the opportunity capital replenishment.

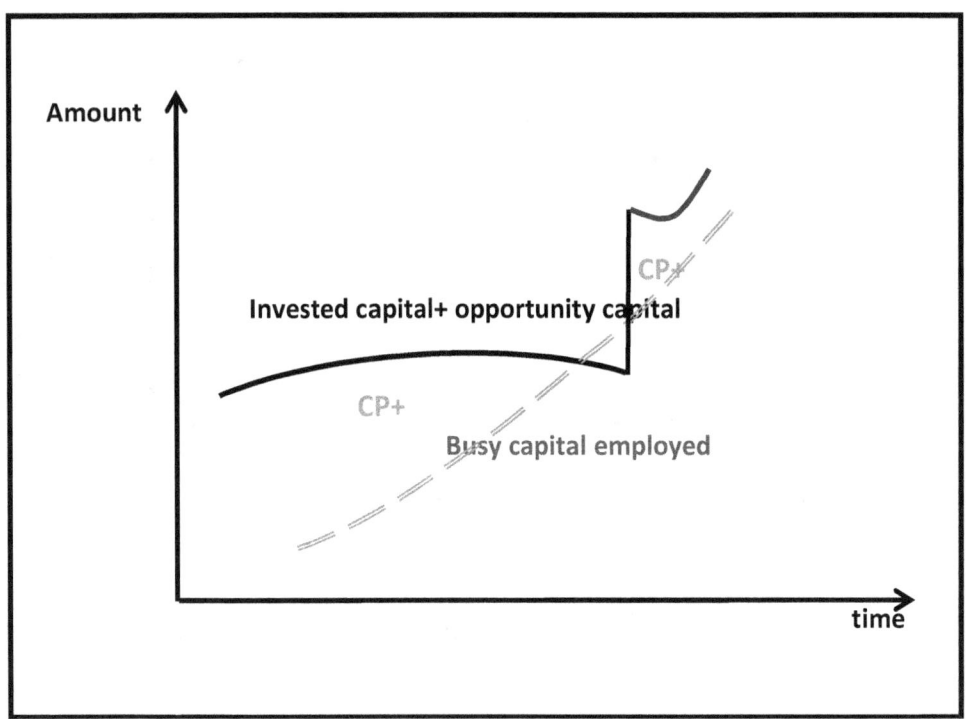

By chance, these events like the Covid crisis are rare.

But, it's the role of the financial manager to consider all types of risk by making his company more anti-fragile.

We have seen that the analysis of a picture at a given date of a financial system is insufficient. The system's evolution is more fruitful, so we need to go further by highlighting the dynamics to create value and cash flows.

This is the subject of the following chapter.

Financial systems dynamics
Key performance indicators

71 The factors of dynamics

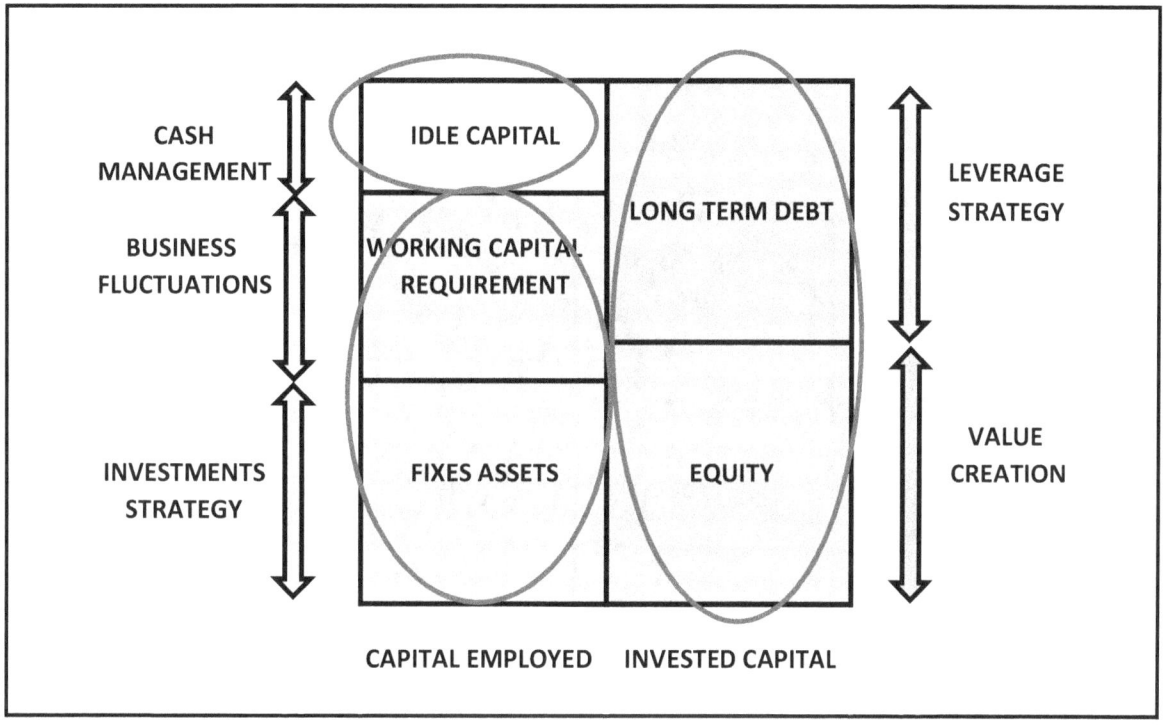

The fluctuations in the financial system play a crucial role in assessing a company's performance and guiding strategic decisions.

The variations of equity drive the process of value creation.
A controlled long-term debt reduces the weighted cost of capital and generates a leverage effect on the return on equity.
The growth of busy capital employed compared with its performance forms the free cash flow.
The level of positive cash position is optimized by the cash management.

In this chapter, we will catch some basic Key Performance Indicators and determine how their intervals generate the main outputs in finance.

Please refer to our book: "The key performance indicators: 88 essentials to understand" available at AMAZON

Financial systems dynamics
Key performance indicators

72 Financial system and value creation

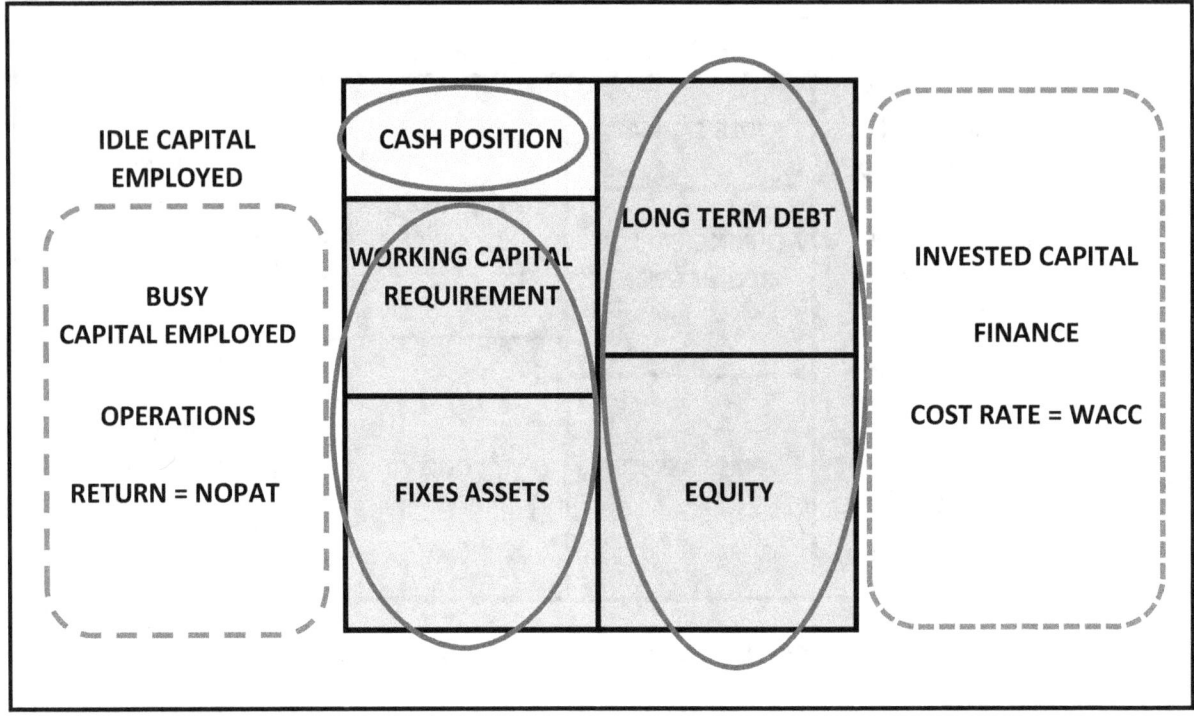

In corporate finance, value creation refers to the process of increasing the worth of the busy capital employed by investing in projects and assets that yield returns greater than their cost of capital.

Financial performance metrics are used to measure value creation. These metrics help assess how well a company is generating profits relative to its invested capital.

The **B**usy **C**apital **E**mployed (**BCE**) to develop and run the business generates an operating profit shown in the profit and loss statement: the **E**arnings **B**efore **I**nterest and **T**ax (**EBIT**).

For consistency, this operating profit is calculated after tax: the **N**et **O**perating **P**rofit **A**fter **T**ax (**NOPAT**).

The **CE** is financed by the invested capital at a rate called **W**eighted **A**verage **C**ost of **C**apital (**WACC**).

Financial systems dynamics
Key performance indicators

The cost of Invested Capital (IC) is: **IC * WACC**

Please refer to our book: "The profit and loss statement: 88 essentials to understand" available at AMAZON

So, the created economic value is the gap between **NOPAT** and **IC*WACC** during a period of time.

Created economic value = **NOPAT – IC*WACC**

The concept of Economic Value Added (**EVA**) was developed by the management consulting firm Stern Stewart & Co. in the 1980s

73 How to improve the economic value creation process?

Looking at the components of the formula, the economic value could be improved if:

- ✓ The NOPAT has a higher efficiency hence the need to set up selective capital budgeting.

- ✓ The invested capital is not wasted meaning a lower busy and idle capital employed thanks to an optimisation of the working capital requirement and of the positive cash position

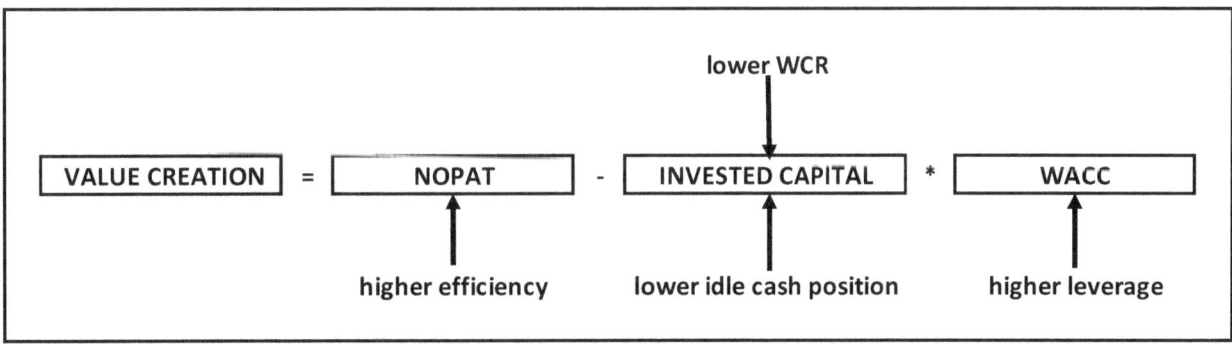

Financial systems dynamics
Key performance indicators

- ✓ The WACC is optimized by dint of a higher use of the long-term debt instead of equity. Indeed, the long-term debt is often cheaper than the cost of equity. This process is called leverage While leverage can amplify returns, it also increases solvency risk (see § 62 page 74). This is why leverage is often described as a double-edged sword.

Outside the optimization of the WACC, the capital budgeting, the cash management and the control of the working capital requirement require a close connection between the financial and the operational management to ensure company's success.

We have noticed that the positive cash position should be minimized but the rule has 2 exceptions:

- ✓ A temporary high positive cash position pending a major investment.

- ✓ A permanent high positive cash position linked to a negative working capital requirement generating an opportunity capital. (see § 59 page 71). The use of the cash position should be restricted the excess over the amount of opportunity capital to avoid the mismatched maturities risk (see § 63 page 77).

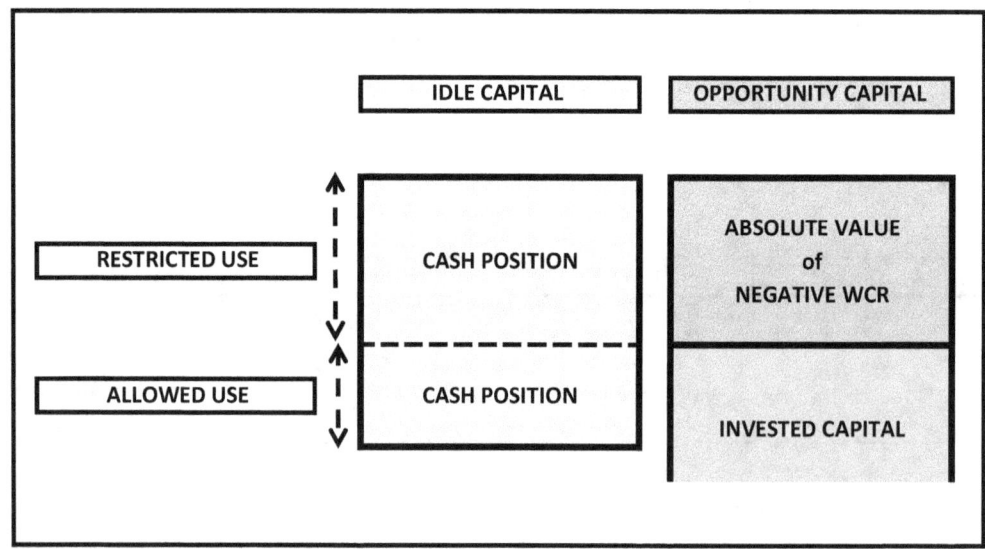

Financial systems dynamics
Key performance indicators

74 Case study

Coming back to the company "marvellous shoes" analysed in § 52 page 60 for which we have built the financial system:

FINANCIAL SYSTEM as of December 31st year N					
CAPITAL EMPLOYED			**INVESTED CAPITAL**		
CP+	90	4,6%	ST FD	290	14,8%
WCR	895	45,7%	LT FD	530	27,1%
FA	974	49,7%	EQUITY	1 139	58,1%
TOTAL	1 959	100,0%	TOTAL	1 959	100,0%

For the next year N+1, we expect a NOPAT of 250 and we would like to calculate the economic value added.

The situation at the end of year N so at the beginning of year N+1 is:

Invested capital (IC) = 1 959

WACC has been calculated for 10 %

So, expected economic value added:
250 – 1 959*10% = 250 – 195,9 = 54,1

First, we notice that an action on the cash position (if permanently at the level of 90) could carry a value added of 90*10% = 9.

But, following the diagnosis seen § 64 page 78, the major action is the lowering of the working capital requirement.
For example, if we can reduce it by 20%, the impact on the value added is 20%*895*10% = 17,9 so an increase of 17,9/54,1 = + 33,1 %

Financial systems dynamics
Key performance indicators

75 Financial system and cash flow

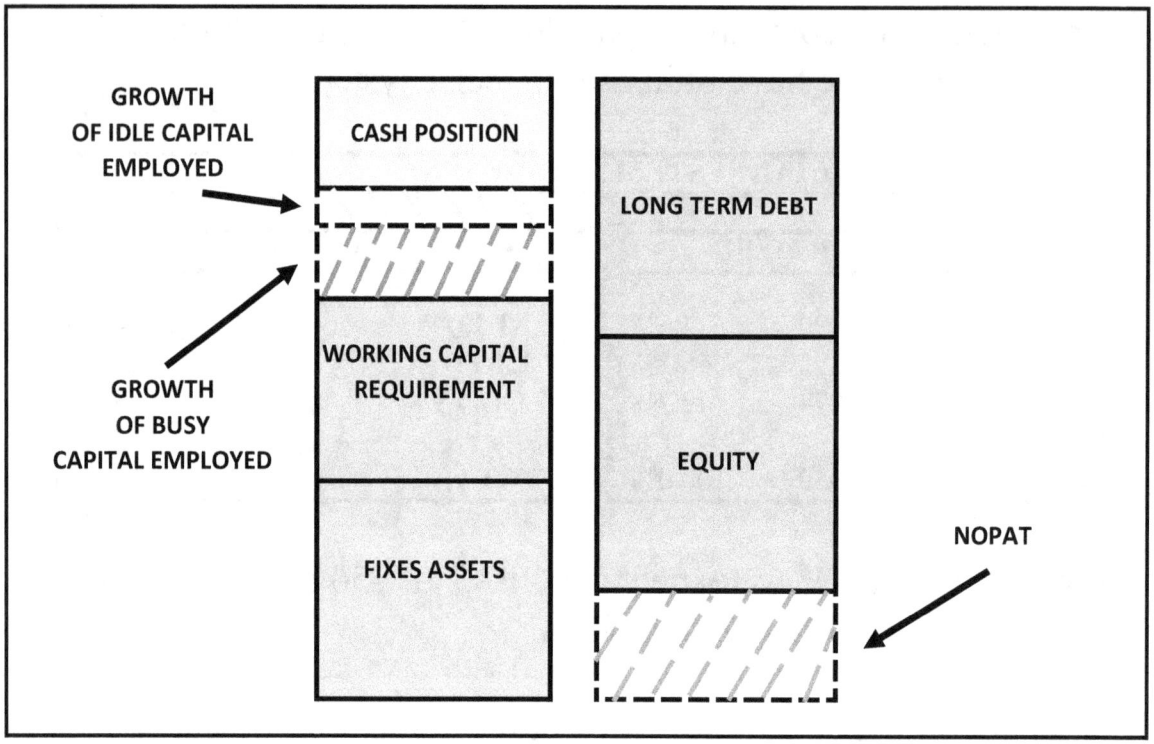

Coming back to the basic equation underlying the financial system:

Busy capital employed + idle capital employed = invested capital

Idle capital employed = invested capital − busy capital employed

The flow of cash is the growth of the positive cash position so the growth of the idle capital employed.

Consequently, flow of cash =

Growth of invested capital − growth of busy capital employed

Financial systems dynamics
Key performance indicators

Let's focus on the **free** cash flow which is the growth of cash caused by current business operations independently of financial and non-recurring events (increase of shareholders capital, payment of dividends, financial expenses, borrowings, loans repayment, non-recurrent operations).

Please refer to our book: "The cash flow statement: 88 essentials to understand" available at AMAZON

With this definition of the free cash flow, the growth of invested capital is limited to the growth of the equity issued from current business operations so the NOPAT.

Free cash flow = NOPAT - growth of busy capital employed

As the busy capital employed is the sum of fixed assets (FA) and working capital requirement (WCR), we write:

Free cash flow = NOPAT – (growth of FA + growth of WCR)

76 the growth rate of busy capital employed vs return

Let's talk about growth rates.
A growth rate measures how much a particular variable changes over a specific period, typically expressed as a percentage. It's used to assess various metrics especially in economy and in finance.
For example, the growth rate of busy capital employed over a period is calculated by following this process:

- ✓ Identify the starting value and the ending value of the variable.
- ✓ Subtract the starting value from the ending value to find the change.
- ✓ Divide the change by the starting value.
- ✓ Multiply by 100 to convert it to a percentage.

Financial systems dynamics
Key performance indicators

So, the **G**rowth **R**ate **O**f busy **C**apital **E**mployed (**GROCE**) over a period is:

$$\frac{\textit{growth of busy capital employed during the period}}{\textit{busy capital employed at the beginning of the period}}$$

This procedure is also used for indicator like the **R**eturn **O**n busy **C**apital **E**mployed (**ROCE**) during an accounting cycle is defined by comparing the **N**et **O**perating **P**rofit **A**fter **T**ax (**NOPAT**) generated during the accounting cycle with the busy **C**apital **E**mployed (**CE0**) at the beginning of the accounting cycle.

$$ROCE = \frac{NOPAT}{CE0}$$

Coming back to the equation last page:

Free cash flow = NOPAT - growth of busy capital employed

If we divide every side of the equation by the starting busy capital employed: CE0

We get: Free cash flow/CE0
=
NOPAT/CE0 – growth of busy capital employed)/CE0

(Free cash flow)/CE0 = ROCE – GROCE

At last:

Free cash flow = CE0 * (ROCE – GROCE)

Financial systems dynamics
Key performance indicators

The free cash flow is generated by the gap between the return on business operations (ROCE) and the growth of the company symbolized by the growth of its busy capital employed.

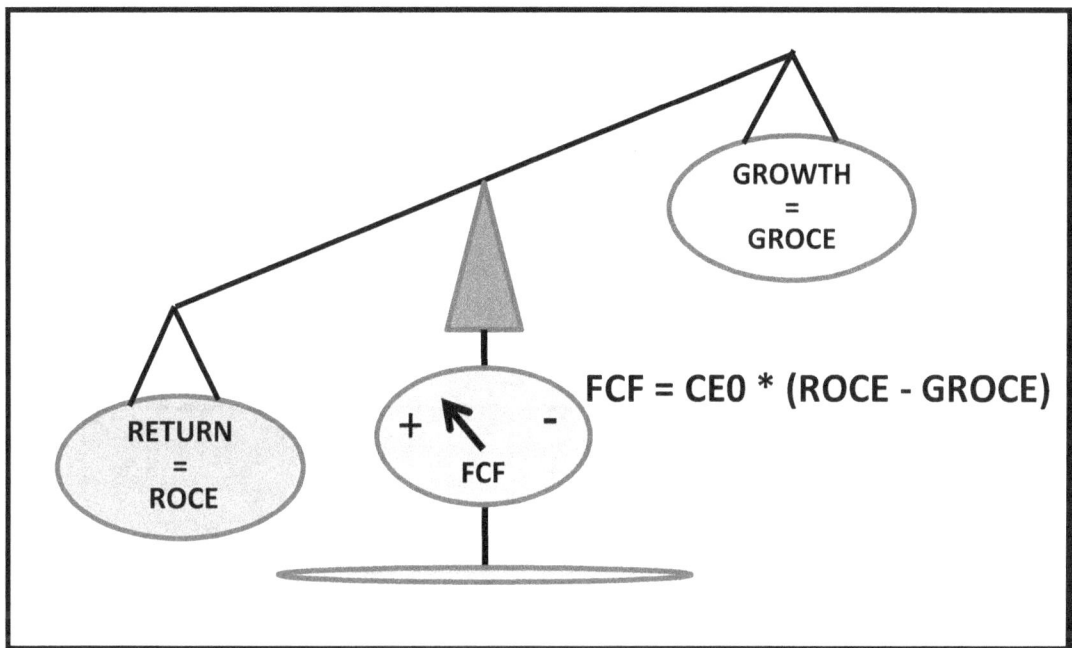

A harmony is necessary between performance and growth

We have seen already in § 67 to 69 pages 81 to 85 that a lack of cash arises from the divergence between invested capital and busy capital employed. (e.g.: a bad performance and/or a too fast growth).

Notice: It also exists another cash flow: the cash surplus available, more comprehensive, which includes the impact of loans variations (financial expenses and repayment), increase of shareholders' capital and payment of dividends.

I invite you to read our book: "The cash flow statement: 88 essentials to understand" available at AMAZON.

Financial systems dynamics
Key performance indicators

77 case study about free cash flow

Let's take again the financial system of "Marvellous shoes" company seen in § 74 page 91

FINANCIAL SYSTEM as of December 31st year N						
CAPITAL EMPLOYED				INVESTED CAPITAL		
CP+	90	4,6%		ST FD	290	14,8%
WCR	895	45,7%		LT FD	530	27,1%
FA	974	49,7%		EQUITY	1 139	58,1%
TOTAL	1 959	100,0%		TOTAL	1 959	100,0%

Free cash flow = CE0 * (ROCE − GROCE)

Busy capital employed end of year N = 895 + 974 = 1 869
Expected ROCE for year N+1 = 250/1 869 = 13, 4 %   (rounded)

Let's calculate the GROCE

Mathematical interlude: (to skip if you have an algebra phobia)

growth rate of busy capital employed
=
(growth of busy capital employed)/ (busy capital employed)
=
(growth of FA + growth of WCR)/ (FA + WCR)
=
{(growth of FA)/ (FA + WCR)} + {(growth of WCR)/ (FA + WCR)}

Multiplying the first factor by FA/FA (so 1) and the second factor by WCR/WCR (so 1) does not change the growth rate of capital employed but gives another look to the equation.

Financial systems dynamics
Key performance indicators

$$\text{growth rate of busy capital employed}$$
$$=$$
$$\{(FA)*(\text{growth of FA})/ (FA)*(FA + WCR)\}$$
$$+$$
$$\{(WCR)*(\text{growth of WCR})/ (WCR)*(FA + WCR)\}$$

Rearranging the two factors gives:

$$\{(FA)/ (FA + WCR) * (\text{growth of FA})/ (FA)\}$$
$$+$$
$$\{(WCR)/ (FA + WCR) * (\text{growth of WCR})/ (WCR)\}$$

(FA)/ (FA + WCR) and (WCR)/ (FA + WCR) are the respective weights of fixed assets and working capital requirement in busy capital employed.
(growth of FA)/ (FA) is the growth rate of fixed assets.
(growth of WCR)/ (WCR) is the growth rate of working capital requirement.

End of mathematical interlude.

GROCE is the weighted average growth rate of the components of the busy capital employed.

The growth rate of fixed assets depends on program of new investments and the depreciation process of former assets.
The growth rate of working capital requirement, at constant inventories turnover and terms of payment, is driven by the company's activity so the increase of sales (refer to § 42 page 48 and § 56 page 66)
For "Marvellous shoes" company:
The expected investment rate program after depreciation is 5 %.
The expected sales are increasing of 10 %

Financial systems dynamics
Key performance indicators

Weight of WCR in busy capital employed = 895/1 869 = 48 %
Weight of FA in busy capital employed = 974/1 869 = 52 %
(Figures are rounded)

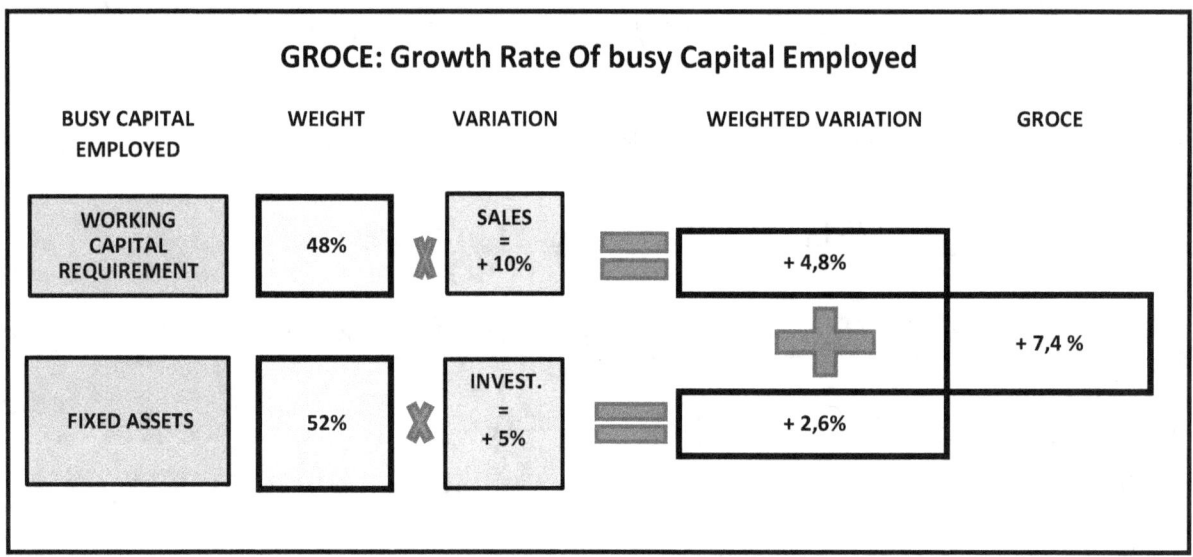

According to the chart above: the expected GROCE = 7,4 %

So, we can calculate:
Expected free cash flow = 1 869 * (13,4 % - 7,4 %) = 52,5

The free cash flow is positive.
It has to cover the obligations linked to the borrowings (financial expenses after tax and repayment of loans) and the distribution of dividends. If not, an additional funding is necessary except if the company has already an excess of cash position.

In conclusion, the free cash flow is driven by only three key numbers: Sales growth, fixed assets growth and the **N**et **O**perating **P**rofit **A**fter **T**ax (NOPAT).

Financial subsystems interdependence interconnections and external impacts

78 financial system interdependence

A system is an integrated entity composed of interconnected subsystems which are self-contained entities. They have their own specific functions but work within the broader context of the main system to contribute to its overall performance and functionality.

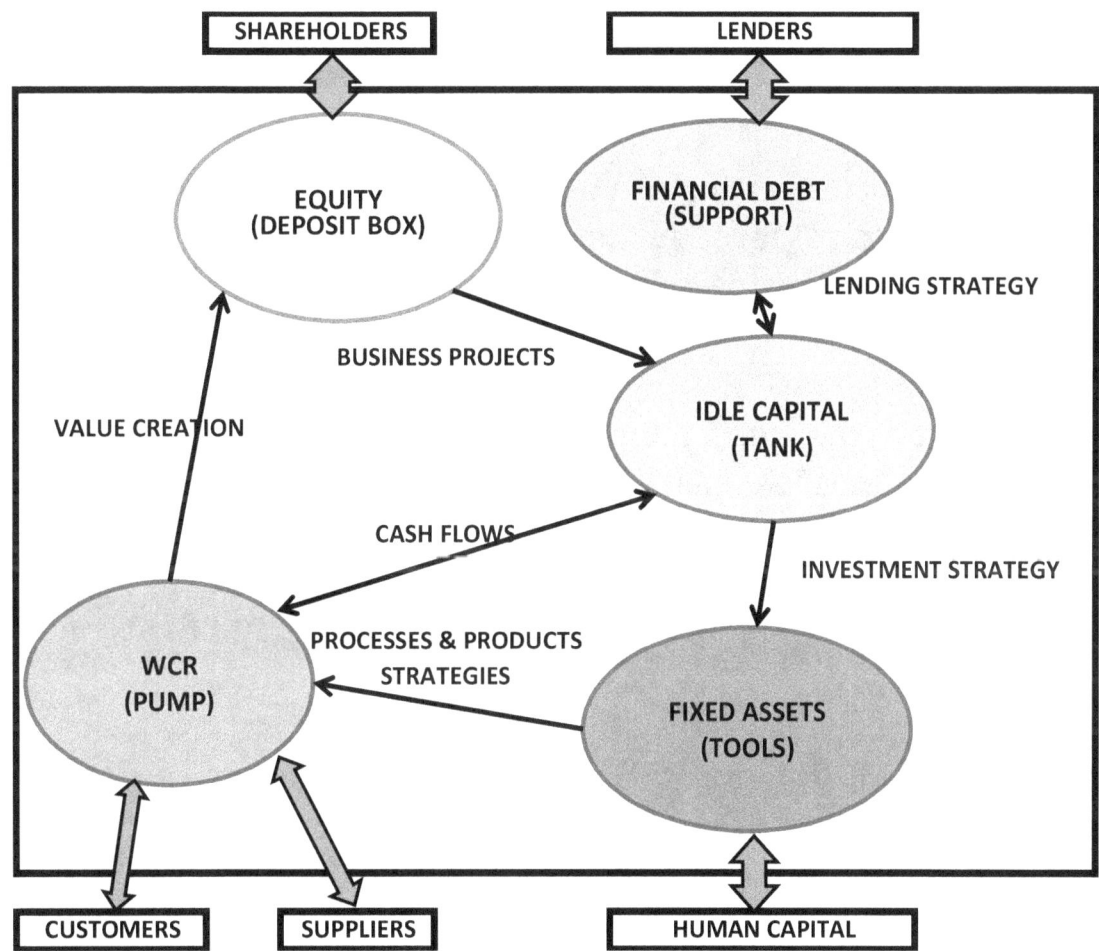

The financial system has 5 subsystems.
The equity which, by its value, is like the company's deposit box.
The financial debt which supports the growth of the company
The idle capital is the tank for cash powered by the working capital requirement as a pump.
The fixed assets, directed by human capital and financed by idle capital, are the tools to create processes and products.

Financial subsystems interdependence interconnections and external impacts

Previously, we have seen the power of the concept of financial system: key variables of the economic value added by comparing the return of one subsystem to the cost of another, or of the free cash flow by the thrust of growing subsystems inside the frame of a financial system balancing capital employed and invested capital.

The analysis of the structure of a financial system also highlights the communications between the subsystems via data nozzles, pathways that transfer data between the different parts.

Conveyed information is of a different nature: business projects, investments, terms payment, processes, ...
The figures in transit are cash flows, revenues and expenses expressed in current currency.

A blockchain can transform the way balance sheets and consequently the financial systems, are managed thanks to a continuous updating of financial transactions.
This generates real-time or past periods financial information allowing company's management to improve decision-making and focus on strategic tasks.

Lack of effectiveness between subsystems can be also revealed:

- ✓ A data inconsistency leading to conflicting or outdated information.
- ✓ A delay or bottleneck in a data nozzle.
- ✓ A malfunction of a critical subsystem impacting the entire system in case of shut down.
- ✓ A gap in communication generating security loopholes and vulnerabilities.

Financial subsystems interdependence interconnections and external impacts

Since we are talking about vulnerabilities, the financial system is a perfect tool to anticipate the impact of external events.

79 financial system and threats

In the table below, we list some economic, fiscal, financial events (the list is not exhaustive) impacting the financial system through its subsystems and their interconnections propagating cascading dysfunctions especially if the threat operates in multiple locations.

A simulation can detect weak points and the extent of the damage on the profitability of the company.

In reaction, it's possible to set up anti-fragility cells which not only oppose the threat but emerge stronger from it.

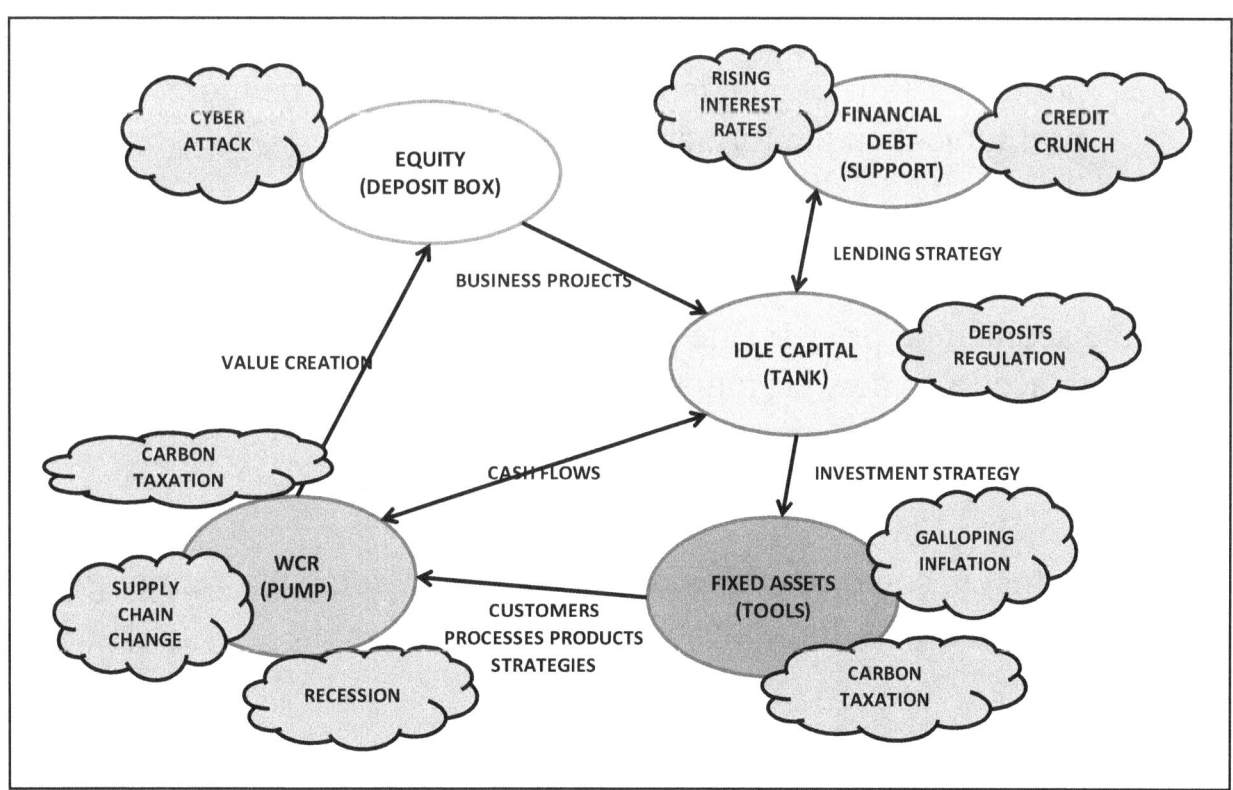

Combinations and consolidated accounting
Definitions

80 Definitions

Different methods are used to combine two or more entities:

- ✓ Merger: a company acquires another company which ceases existing to become part of the acquiring company.

- ✓ Acquisition: the acquiring company (called parent company) obtains control (full or partial) of the acquired company (the daughter company) but both companies keep their structure and are combined in a third entity called "group".

- ✓ Consolidation: A new company is especially created to consolidate the assets and the liabilities of 2 companies. Their shareholders receive in exchange common shares of the new company. (On the contrary, a spinoff is the creation of an independent company from the division of another company hoping that the new independent company will be more profitable than the former division).

81 Why create a group?

In the acquisition process, the parent company wants to grow in size, to have access to new customers, to expand into new countries but by investing less money by taking only a partial control of acquired companies.

(Notice that in some countries, a foreign parent company cannot get the full control of a domestic company).

Combinations and consolidated accounting
Definitions

82 The consolidated financial statements

The group has not a legal existence but it's a way to enhance a brand name and to boost the branding of products all over the world.

However, in financial accounting, the different acquisitions are accounted:

- In the balance sheet of the parent company as financial investments without disclosing their assets and liabilities,
- In the profit and loss statement as dividends without disclosing their sales and costs.

That's why, it is more accurate (and mandatory for listed companies) to aggregate the financial statements of a group of companies owned partially or fully by a parent company.

These financial statements are called consolidated financial statements (don't make a confusion with the process of consolidation in § 80)

83 Control versus ownership

- ✓ The ownership defines the level of stake the parent company (as a shareholder) in the daughter company.

- ✓ The control means the capacity of the parent company to manage and decide in the daughter company.

Theoretically, if the shareholders have the majority of votes, they can exercise the full control of the company but practically this situation suffers many exceptions.

Combinations and consolidated accounting
Definitions

In the consolidation process, the percentage of control defines the scope and selects the method while the percentage of ownership is used to aggregate some items of the group statements.

84 Scope and methods of consolidation

The scope of consolidation is the list of entities including:

- ✓ The parent company
- ✓ The companies hold directly or indirectly by the parent company at the level of at least 20 % of control

The financial statements of the companies inside the scope are aggregated with the financial statements of the parent company according to techniques explained further.

The companies outside the scope but hold by the parent company are represented in its balance sheet at their historical cost of acquisition in the section "investments" of fixed assets.

There are 2 techniques of consolidation:

- ✓ Full consolidation
- ✓ Equity consolidation

85 Full consolidation method

This technique is used if the parent company has the full control of its daughter company.
The full control is supposed to exist if the parent company holds directly or indirectly at least 50 % of the control of its daughter.
In this case, 100 % of assets and liabilities of the daughter company are aggregated to the balance sheet of the parent company.

Combinations and consolidated accounting
Definitions

The line "investment" showing the stake of the parent company in the daughter company is eliminated.

A line "goodwill" appears in intangible assets of the group if the stake of the parent company was valued **at the date of acquisition** for a price higher than the book value of the daughter company computed in proportion of the percentage of ownership of the parent company.

100 % of assets and liabilities of the daughter company are recorded with the assets and the liabilities of the parent company to form the assets and liabilities of the group.

The change between the line "investment" valued at the date of acquisition and the book value of the daughter company **at the date of consolidation** computed in proportion of the percentage of ownership of the parent company is recorded in the equity of the group as "portion of retained earnings of fully consolidated companies".

The percentage of ownership, not belonging to the parent company, is applied to the book value of the daughter company **at the date of consolidation** to compute the line "minority interests on the right-hand side of the balance sheet of the group.

Notice: Some additional adjustments are necessary: elimination of intra group transactions (loans, dividends payable ...), translation of foreign entities accounts in the currency of the parent company etc....

86: The equity consolidation method

This technique is used if the parent company has a "significant influence" on its daughter company.
The significant influence is supposed to exist if the parent company controls directly or indirectly less than 50 % its daughter company (but at least 20 % to be in the scope of consolidation).

Combinations and consolidated accounting
Definitions

In this case, assets and liabilities of the daughter company are not aggregated to the balance sheet of the parent company to form the group.

The line "investment" showing the stake of the parent company in the daughter company is recalculated according to the book value of the daughter company at the date of consolidation and named "investment in equity consolidated companies".

The change between the line "investment" valued at the historical cost at the date of acquisition and the new line "investment in equity consolidated companies" valued at the date of consolidation is recorded in the equity of the parent company as "portion of retained earnings of equity consolidated companies".

Two case studies below will help you to understand the concept of consolidation.

Combinations and consolidated accounting
Case studies

87 Example of full consolidation:

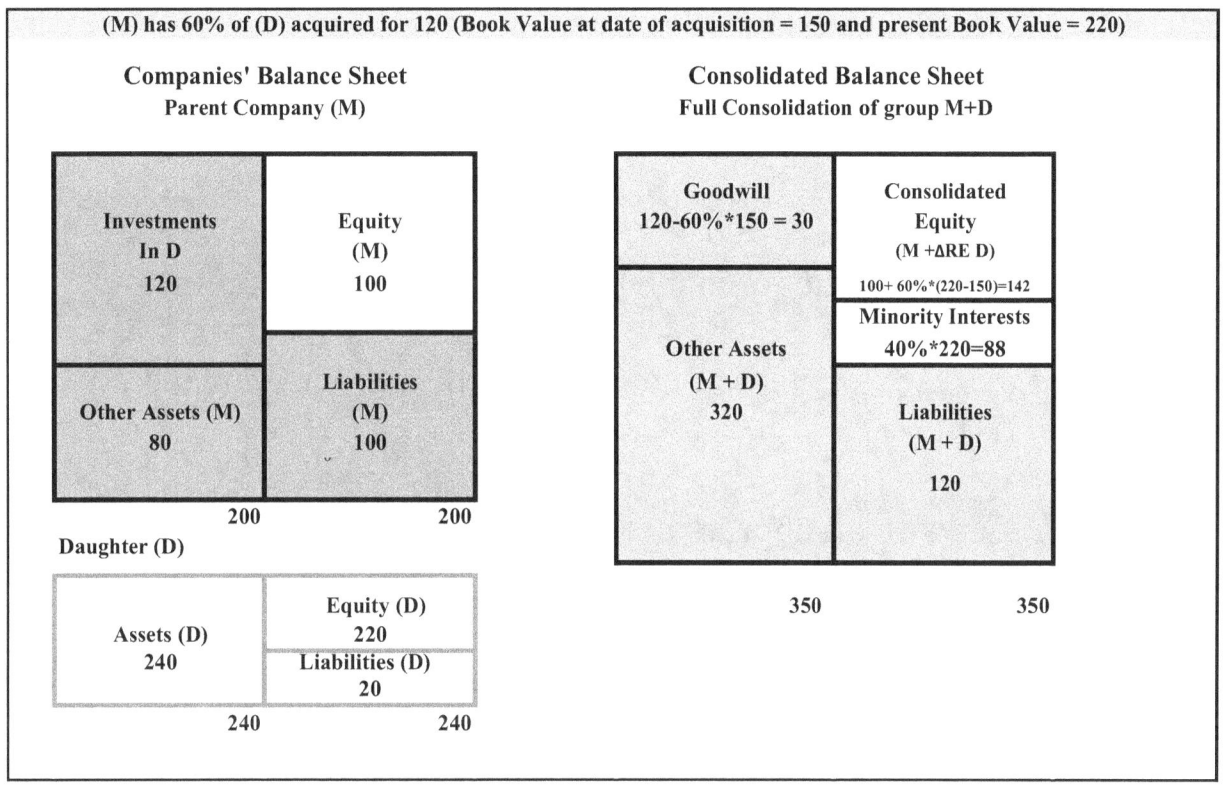

The parent company (**M**) owns 60 % of another company (called the daughter company (**D**)).

Here, we have a direct link between the parent and the daughter so we can suppose that the percentage of ownership (60%) is also the percentage of control.

With such a percentage, the daughter company (**D**) is in the scope of consolidation of the parent and the method of consolidation to be used is the full consolidation method.

The cost of acquisition of the 60 % is 120 recorded in the line "investments" in the fixed assets of the parent company.

Combinations and consolidated accounting
Case studies

At the time of acquisition, the book value (the equity) of the daughter company (**D**) was 150.

The parent company (**M**) has paid 120 to acquire 60 % of 150 so 60%*150= 90.

The excess of price 120 – 90 = 30 paid by the parent company can be explained by the quality of management of the daughter company (Research, marketing, experience of managers …) and cannot be allocated to a specific item of the balance sheet of the daughter company (**D**).

Named "goodwill", it appears in the consolidated balance sheet of the group in the line "intangible asset".

The line "investments" for 120 in the mother company (**M**) is eliminated in the consolidated balance sheet and replaced by a line "goodwill" for 30.

Then, we record in the consolidated balance sheet 100 % of assets and liabilities of the daughter company with the assets and liabilities of the parent company.

Notice: Assets and liabilities are ranked without distinction of the original company under the right item in the consolidated balance sheet (**M+D**).
So, we have a total of assets of 350 on the left hand-side.

For the right-hand side we have a sum of liabilities of 120.

For the equity of the group, we add to the equity of the parent (**M**) 100, the increase of equity (book value) of the daughter company (**D**) since the date of acquisition in proportion of the percentage of ownership 60%.

Combinations and consolidated accounting
Case studies

So, 60 %*(220 -150) = 42 and for a total equity of (**M+D**) = 142

In full consolidation, we aggregate 100 % of assets and liabilities of the daughter company (**D**) even if the parent company (**M**) owns less, so we have to show in the consolidated balance sheet of the group (**M+D**) the value of the daughter company (**D**) belonging to outsiders of the group called "minority interests".

In this example, the value of the daughter company (**D**) owned by minority interests is calculated as:

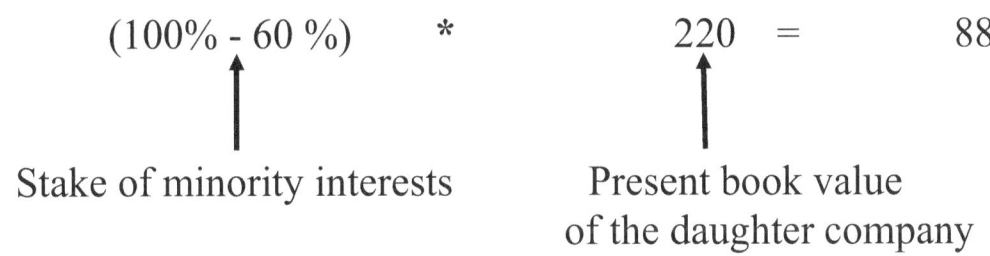

(100% - 60 %)   *   220   =   88

Stake of minority interests   Present book value of the daughter company

The minority interests are recorded in long-term debt (IFRS rules) or in equity section (US GAAP rules).

We have a total for liabilities + equity: 120 + 142 + 88 = 350

- ✓ Consolidated liabilities = 120
- ✓ Consolidated equity = 142
- ✓ Minority interests = 88

The consolidated balance sheet (**M+D**) is balanced.

Combinations and consolidated accounting
Case studies

88 Example of equity consolidation

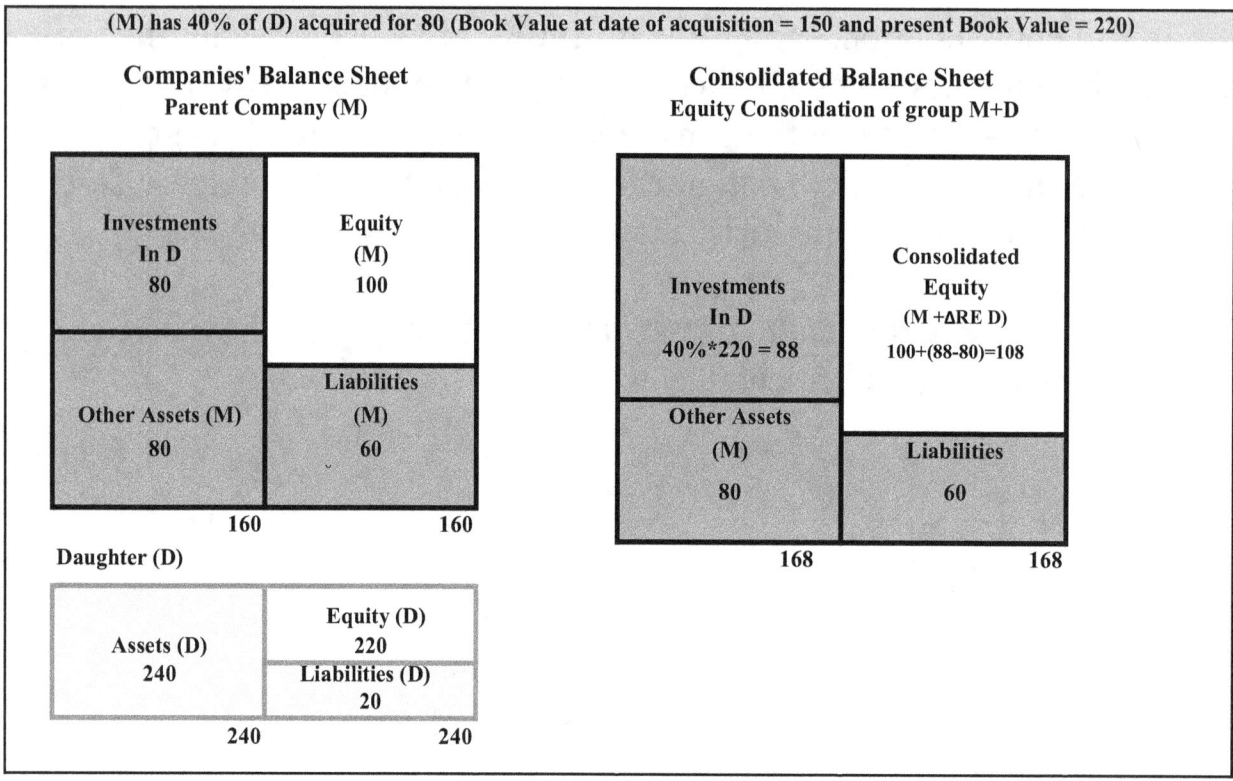

We take the same parent (**M**) and daughter (**D**) companies as seen above but the parent company (**M**) has only acquired 40 % of the daughter company (**D**).

With such a percentage, the daughter company (**D**) is still in the scope of consolidation of the parent (**M**) but the method of consolidation to be used is the equity consolidation method.

The consolidated balance sheet of the group will only aggregate the assets and the liabilities of the parent company (**M**) but the investment in the daughter (**D**) will be replaced by the value of its equity in proportion of the percentage of ownership.

Combinations and consolidated accounting
Case studies

$$40\% \quad * \quad 220 \quad = \quad 88$$

Stake of the mother company   Present book value
of the daughter company

We have for the assets of the group (**M+D**) a total of 168:

Assets of the parent company (**M**) = 160 + variance of value of investment in the daughter company (**D**) = (88 – 80) = 8

For the right-hand side, liabilities and equity of the group (**M+D**):
60 + 100 + 8 = 168

- ✓ Liabilities of the parent company (**M**) = 60
- ✓ Equity of the parent company (**M**) = 100
- ✓ Variance of the investment in the daughter company (**D**) = 8

The consolidated balance sheet (**M+D**) is balanced.

Conclusion

I hope you have enjoyed this explanation of the balance sheet's secrets.

I remind you my other books useful to understand different aspects in corporate finance and financial accounting available at Amazon.

- ✓ "The profit and loss statement: 88 essentials to understand"
- ✓ "The cashflow statement: 88 essentials to understand" (published in November 2024)
- ✓ "The key performance indicators: 88 essentials to understand" (published in January 2025)
- ✓ "The 88 essentials MBA student must know in financial accounting"
- ✓ "The 88 essentials an entrepreneur must know in finance to run successfully a business"
- ✓ "The 88 essentials you must know if you are a neophyte in financial accounting and corporate finance"

Si vous êtes francophone, je vous propose aussi : "La finance d'entreprise pour les nuls" publié chez FIRST Editions.

More information on our website: www.mycampusfinance.com

Any question? Please contact us: mycampusfinance@gmail.com

www.ingramcontent.com/pod-product-compliance
Lightning Source LLC
Chambersburg PA
CBHW062219220526
45471CB00009B/3261